# LOVE
## THE ULTIMATE
## APOLOGETIC

### The Heart of Christian Witness

## Art Lindsley

IVP Books

An imprint of InterVarsity Press
Downers Grove, Illinois

*InterVarsity Press*
*P.O. Box 1400, Downers Grove, IL 60515-1426*
*World Wide Web: www.ivpress.com*
*E-mail: email@ivpress.com*

*InterVarsity Press® is the book-publishing division of InterVarsity Christian Fellowship/USA®, a student movement active on campus at hundreds of universities, colleges and schools of nursing in the United States of America, and a member movement of the International Fellowship of Evangelical Students. For information about local and regional activities, write Public Relations Dept., InterVarsity Christian Fellowship/USA, 6400 Schroeder Rd., P.O. Box 7895, Madison, WI 53707-7895, or visit the IVCF website at <www.intervarsity.org>.*

*Design: Cindy Kiple*
*ISBN 978-0-8308-3427-3*

*Printed in the United States of America* ∞

**Library of Congress Cataloging-in-Publication Data**

*Lindsley, Arthur.*
  *Love, the ultimate apologetic: the heart of Christian witness / by*
*Art Lindsley.*
    *p. cm.*
  *Includes bibliographical references (p. ) and index.*
  *ISBN 978-0-8308-3427-3 (pbk.: alk. paper)*
  *1. Love—Religious aspects—Christianity. 2. Apologetics. I.*
*Title.*
*BV4639.L496 2008*
*241'.4—dc22*

                                          *2008002179*

| P | 19 | 18 | 17 | 16 | 15 | 14 | 13 | 12 | 11 | 10 | 9 | 8 | 7 | 6 | 5 | 4 | 3 | 2 | 1 |
|---|----|----|----|----|----|----|----|----|----|----|----|----|----|----|----|----|----|----|----|
| Y | 24 | 23 | 22 | 21 | 20 | 19 | 18 | 17 | 16 | 15 | 14 | 13 | 12 | 11 | 10 | 09 | 08 | | | |

*To Arthur and Lois,*

*my Mom and Dad,*

*who taught and demonstrated to me*

*Jesus' truth, justice and love*

# CONTENTS

# ACKNOWLEDGMENTS

I am indebted to the many people who helped me in the writing of this book. First, I want to thank the staff of Westmont College for inviting me to be a visiting professor during the summers and allowing me the use of their facilities. I particularly want to thank Provost Shirley Mullen, President Stan Gaede and library director John Murray. My utmost gratitude goes to Dale and Sandy Larsen for their skillful editing of this manuscript, which immensely improved the book.

I owe a special thanks to Becky Cooke for preparing the manuscript through its many drafts and for all the time she freely donated to this project. Special thanks also go to many faithful donors who made this project possible: Mrs. Frank Alling, Bill and Rosemary Bailey, Bob and Jean Baldwin, Otis Bowden, Ken and Caroline Broussard, Harland and Sheila Buhler, Jim and Mary Beth Carroll, Jim and Becky Cooke, Kim and Kathy Cooke, Richard and Robin Drew, Gil and Ruth Emery, Stuart and Judy Graydon, Bob and Martha Haley, David Hinshelwood, Jim and Lorraine Hiskey, Dennis and Karen Hogge, Shang Hsiung, Jack and Joanne Kemp, Carl and Kay Meyer, Joan Miers, John and Alex Mitchell, Kerry and Debora Moody, Bill and Marsha Nickels, Todd and Pam Ramsey, Rick and Sharon Schatz, Michael and Diana Schick, Dick and Nancy Schultze, Oliver and Julia Thomas, Wendy Verhof, Rick and Dody Wellock, and Caz Zimmer.

I am also thankful for those who willingly read the manuscript and gave comments: Byron Beck, Bill and Debbie Cron, Stuart Graydon, Kemp Gouldin, and Dave Thompson. My InterVarsity Press editor, Gary Deddo, has been a pleasure to work with yet again.

Last, but not least, I want to thank my wife, Connie, who encouraged me in my writing and occupied our boys, giving me focused time to invest in completing the book. Thanks to Trey and Jon for allowing their dad the time to write and to read to them sections of the book. Your interest and questions encouraged me to finish the project.

# HOW WILL THEY KNOW?

## They Will Know Us
## by Our Love

*From his vantage point in a corner of the bookstore coffee shop, John
scans the people lined up to buy coffee or tea, muffins or bagels. He
rests his hand on his Bible and silently wonders,* Who's going to show
up this time?

*For the next seven weeks, John will lead a discussion about a basic
human experience and need: love.* Everybody is interested in love,
John muses. I hope we get a wide variety of viewpoints, like we had
before.

*John smiles as he recalls the people he met in this same spot to discuss
the writings of C. S. Lewis.*[1] *Now he sees one of them, Simon, turn away
from the counter and look around. John waves. Simon can't wave back
because he's holding a mug in one hand and a bagel in the other hand,
but he nods and heads toward John's table. John can't help thinking,* He
looks so conservative for a person with such nonconformist ideas.

*"Do I really need a nametag?" Simon asks as he surveys the sticky
labels and marker. "You know me—Simon the atheist." Both John and
Simon can now laugh at the designation. Simon had begun the previous study taut and defensive. Over the weeks, though, he let down his
guard somewhat and became less absolute in his opinions. When John*

*last spoke to him, Simon at least seemed open to exploring the possibility of God. And he's shown up for this group, which should count for something.*

*John has barely explained, "We may have some new people this time," when a very familiar person appears. It's Julia, making her usual flamboyant entrance.*

*"Hel-lo, Simon. Hel-lo, John. So good to see you again!" She sets down her mug of steaming tea and starts to fill out a nametag. "I can't wait to get into this discussion about love. If we would just learn to walk in the way of love, it would solve so many problems in the world."*

*Simon asks, "So, are you still on your spiritual quest?"*

*Julia looks surprised. "Of course. The quest is never-ending. We never stop learning until we die, and then we just move into a higher plane of experience. Don't you agree? Oh, that's right, you don't believe in Spirit, do you?" Julia is deeply committed to her own brand of spirituality, an eclectic blend of Eastern religions and New Age beliefs. She finishes printing her name with a flourish and sticks the label on her brightly printed blouse.*

*Julia is just getting settled when an older man arrives. He nods at everyone. "This must be the place."*

*"Hi, Mike!" The others quickly shift their chairs to make room for the newcomer. John adds, "It's good to see you again." Mike was the oldest in the C. S. Lewis discussion group and the one closest to John's own Christian beliefs.*

*Mike sits down and peers at his thick, white coffee cup. "They're making these mugs smaller all the time."*

*Simon deadpans, "Maybe your hands are getting bigger." Everyone laughs. It's the sort of remark Mike himself usually makes.*

*John glances at his watch, and Julia looks around. "Is this all we're going to have?" Soon her question is answered. A very young woman* hurries into the coffee shop looking around in all directions. She spots the group and makes a beeline for them. "Is this the discussion group about love?" she asks. When everyone nods, she says, "Hi, I'm Annette. I saw the flyer, and I'm really interested in this topic." She starts to sit down, then quickly stands up again. "Can you wait a sec? I've just got to get some coffee." She hurries away toward the counter.

Julia asks, "How did she know we were the discussion group?"

"By our smiling faces?" John suggests.

Mike shakes his head and leans over the table confidentially. "By our nametags."

Annette is back. John introduces everyone at the table, then he pulls his own coffee mug a little closer. "As you know, our purpose in these next seven weeks is to focus on the subject of love. In particular we're going to look at Jesus Christ's teaching about love and what makes it unique. Annette, I don't want to put you on the spot, but you said you were especially interested in this subject. Would you mind saying why?"

Immediately Annette loses her rather harried look. Her face lights up. "My boyfriend, Richard, and I are ready to take our relationship to the next level. And we've started going to this church near where we live. We really like it—they've got a lot of things for people our age. I've done some reading in the Bible, and I like what it says about love."

Julia looks directly at John. "Well, that raises my first question. All religions teach love. So why do we have to narrow this down to Jesus Christ?"

John smiles. "Because that's what the brochure says. But it's actually a good question," he adds as Julia opens her mouth to protest. "When we take a look at love from a Christian viewpoint, I think we'll find an interesting contrast between Jesus' teachings and other systems of belief."

Julia frowns and muses. "Other systems of belief. There must be thousands. No—billions. Every person has his or her own belief system."

*Annette protests, "How long is this going to last? I thought it was only for seven weeks. I can't commit to longer than seven weeks."*

*John says, "Julia's right. There's no way to consider every possible idea about love—which is why I've chosen to use one as a basis for comparison with others. I think Jesus is an interesting place to start because he made an extreme statement about how his followers can be recognized. He said people will know they are Christians by their love for each other."*

*"And we all believe that."*

*John lets Simon's sarcastic statement sink in for a moment. The group members glance around nervously, but no one says anything, so John continues. "We'll consider love from the viewpoint of atheism, which says that everything is matter, and from the viewpoint of pantheism, which says that everything is spirit."* He shifts a little in his chair. He knows his next statement will stir people up. *"I'm going to maintain that atheists and pantheists find it difficult, if not impossible, to discover an adequate basis for love."*

*Simon sits up straighter. "So you're saying I can't be loving if I don't believe in God?"*

*John responds quickly. "I'm not saying you personally are unloving or even that atheists in general are unloving."* Don't get defensive, he reminds himself. *"I'm just saying there's nothing in the atheist view of life that* requires *or* sustains *love for other people."*

*Simon looks like he's about to answer, but Julia speaks up again. "You're talking like all Christians are full of love. But that's just not true. I mean, just look at history. Christians have shown a lot of hatred, especially for people of other religions."*

*"Yeah, like the Crusades," Annette adds. "And the way some Christians think all Muslims are terrorists."*

*John admits, "Good point. G. K. Chesterton said the best argument against Christianity is Christians. But he also said the best argument* for *Christianity is Christians. I believe we can find a lot of examples of believers through the centuries demonstrating Christ's love, even to people of other religions."*

*"And great examples of the opposite," Simon insists.*

*"That's right. But at least there's a good explanation for why some Christians don't live up to their beliefs. Christians don't claim that the good people are in church and the bad people are outside of it. They say we are all sinners who need a Savior."*

*"You said something about—what was it?—pantheism?" Mike puts in. "I'm not even sure what that is."*

*John explains, "A pantheist believes that all is one, that everything is God."*

*Julia nods vigorously. "That's what I believe!"*

*John goes on. "The popular form that pantheism takes in our culture is New Age spirituality, drawing from Eastern religions. Julia, I think that's where you'd done most of your spiritual searching." He smiles. "That is, until you came here."*

*"You said something about sinners," Julia returns, and John wonders if she is dodging his last comment. "I hate that whole Christian idea of sin. You know—this person's good, this other person's bad. I think we are all already perfect if we just realize it."*

*"So where does love fit into all that?" Simon asks. "We're talking about love here, aren't we?"*

*"Well, if we're all part of the whole, then everything is already together in love and harmony," Julia explains. "I believe in love toward all Being—toward the One."*

*There's a brief silence before Mike comments, "Sounds to me like you love 'Being' in general, but you don't love anybody in particular."*

*John jumps in. "Let's hold off on any more discussion until we take a look at the Bible passage for this week."*

## ATHEIST ON A TRAIN

Like some members of the study group, many people have the impression that all worldviews and religions equally encourage love. It may come as a surprise that they do not. The idea for this book started when I was speaking in Eastern Europe and Russia on cults and world religions. On a train ride from Vienna, Austria, to Budapest, Hungary, my wife and I sat in a car with four other people. Two of them were atheists, and the other two had at least some church background. As we talked, we discovered that one of our traveling companions was a believer who was the nephew of a prominent leader in the Christian community. The uncle had faced many difficult relational struggles in his ministry. We talked about the difficulty of relationships and the unique way Christ calls us to forgive and to love.

One of the atheists, a young man, shared his desire for a loving marriage and family. He asked, "Can't atheists love and forgive?"

I responded, "Yes, of course atheists can love and forgive, but not because of their atheism."

A lengthy discussion ensued along these lines. In the atheist perspective, all is matter. There is no God, no solid basis for moral values other than individual and community preference, and no source for the other-centered agape love that Christ embodies and teaches his followers to practice.

Atheism leads inevitably to a grim and meaningless universe. It encourages autonomy rather than love. Atheist philosopher Bertrand Russell held that since God does not exist, we need to build our lives on the basis of "unyielding despair." Fellow atheist and existential philosopher Albert Camus said that the only really serious question is whether or not to commit suicide. Fyodor Dostoyevsky had a character in one of his novels argue that if there is no God, everything is permitted. Another atheist, Jean Paul Sartre, said that no finite point has meaning without an infinite reference point; and since life has no infinite reference point, life is therefore meaningless. Sartre said that it does not matter whether you choose to help an old lady across the street or beat her over the head; in either case, just be authentic.

Where in atheism is there any basis or motive for love and forgiveness? If anything, atheism undermines love and forgiveness. Certainly atheists often love their spouses, their children and other people, but not because atheism encourages love or because love is a necessary consequence of atheism.

Throughout the conversation on the train, our young atheist companion followed each point and admitted that he had never thought about this before.

I went on to point out that love is at the core of Jesus' message. We live in a universe where personality is valued over impersonal matter. God is personal; in fact God is *tripersonal*—Father, Son and Holy Spirit. Personality is at the core of the cosmos. The Persons of the Trinity are in an eternal relationship of love. So love and relationship are at the center of reality. God has made humanity in his image. We are given worth, value and dignity that can never be taken away from us. Furthermore, we are made in the likeness of God to express our God-given personalities, engage in relationships, and love God and other people.

Jesus placed love at the center in his summation of the Old Testament law. When asked which is the greatest commandment, Jesus replied, "Love the Lord your God with all your heart and with all your soul and with all your mind" (Matthew 22:37). Then he added, "And the second is like it: 'Love your neighbor as yourself'" (Matthew 22:39).

On the night before he was crucified, Jesus gave an additional exhortation: "A new command I give you: Love one another. As I have loved you, so you must love one another" (John 13:34). He went on to make this kind of love the mark of discipleship. Love is the evidence and confirmation by which people can know that these are Jesus' followers: "By this everyone will know that you are my disciples, if you have love for one another" (John 13:35 NRSV). Jesus went so far as to say, "Love your enemies and pray for those who persecute you" (Matthew 5:44).

Besides his commands to love others, Jesus also called his followers to radical forgiveness, to forgive "seventy-seven times" (Matthew 18:22). Forgiveness was so important to Jesus that after he gave his disciples what we call the Lord's Prayer, he laid down these extreme conditions: "If you forgive others their trespasses, your heavenly Father will also forgive you; but if you do not forgive others, neither will your Father forgive your trespasses" (Matthew 6:14-15 NRSV).

I gave the young atheist on the train a summary of the above ideas. Then I put this question to him: "Which view do you think gives an adequate basis for love and forgiveness—atheism or faith in Christ?" He readily admitted that it wasn't atheism, and he seemed fascinated by these new insights. At that moment we arrived at the border of Hungary, where this man found out that as a Canadian he did not have the visa necessary to enter the country, and border guards escorted him off the train. We made plans to meet him in Budapest the next day, but he didn't make it. I have often wondered what happened to this honest, open young atheist.

## ATHEISTIC HUMANISM

Some atheists hold to a form of humanism. Although they maintain that humanity originated out of matter, time and chance, and although our destiny is oblivion with no life after death, they believe that somehow human beings are significant.

Some atheists say that our origin is insignificant, that our destiny is "full of sound and fury signifying nothing" and that people are merely a "useless passion." In fact, Sartre wrote in his play *No Exit,* "Hell is other people." For an atheist, human origin, existence and destiny are nothing but big zeros.

Humanistic atheists concede that humanity emerged spontaneously out of the cosmic slime and that even the noblest person eventually rots in the grave. Yet somehow, in spite of the fact that humans came from nothing and are going nowhere, these atheists still believe that humans are a great big plus. It is a noble-sounding affirmation, but humanists have no basis for ascribing dignity to human beings. Perhaps they know in their consciences that human beings are valuable, because God's law is "written on their hearts" (Romans 2:15). Psychologist Erik Erickson once made the comment that he could think of no other reason to assign humans dignity than that they are made in the image of God. From an atheistic standpoint, there is no sufficient reason why we ought to treat humans with such value. There appears to be no intrinsic basis for an atheist to encourage love and forgiveness.

|  | Origin | Humanity | Destiny |
|---|---|---|---|
| Atheism | O | O | O |
| Humanism | O | + | O |
| Christianity | + | + | + |

An article in the *Wall Street Journal* titled "In Europe God Is (Not) Dead" notes a prominent thinker's observation:

Jürgen Habermas, influential German intellectual, member of the originally Marxist Frankfurt School of philosophy and self-described "methodical atheist," has revised his view that modernization inevitably leads to secularization. In a 2004 book, *Time of Transitions,* he hailed Christianity as the bedrock of Western values: "Christianity, and nothing else, is the ultimate foundation of liberty, conscience, human rights, and democracy, the benchmarks of Western civilization. To this day, we have no other options [than Christianity]. We continue to nourish ourselves from this source. Everything else is postmodern chatter."[2]

In contrast to atheism, Christianity argues that God is the origin of life and that human beings are made in his image. Therefore, we have intrinsic worth and dignity based not on what we do but on who we are. Because of a loving Creator, we have value, our lives matter and our destiny is eternal, either for salvation or for judgment.

## ALL IS ONE?

If atheists find no solid basis for love in a universe where "all is matter," followers of New Age spirituality find no firmer foundation for love in a universe where "all is spirit."

There are many forms of Hinduism and Buddhism. I will focus on what might be called *absolute pantheism,* as exemplified by the Hindu philosopher Shankara and others who hold similar views. This perspective, as it has come through to the New Age movement in the West, holds that "all is One." Marilyn Ferguson, in her classic book *The Aquarian Conspiracy,* points out that the negative way to express this positive principle is *nondistinction.*[3] There are no real distinctions anywhere. Matter, time, space, cause and effect are all illusory.

A second related principle is that humans are divine. Since we are part of the One, we are in a sense *gods* or *divine*. Note that the One is not a personal being but an impersonal force—an it rather than a he or she. We may be part of it, but it cannot value us, love us or forgive us.

A third implication of New Age beliefs is that the purpose of our existence is to alter our consciousness so we come to see that there are no real distinctions in this world. We need to transcend this illusory world and realize that all is One. Only then will we be able to achieve unlimited power to create our own reality. The only limit to what we can do is our own imagination.

Other advocates affirm the all-is-One, nondistinct philosophy. For example, Deepak Chopra writes in his bestseller *The Seven Spiritual Laws of Success,* "The physical universe is nothing other than the Self curving back within Itself to experience Itself."[4] In the same context, he writes that there are "seeds of divinity within us" and that we are "divinity in disguise."[5] In Chopra's book *Ageless Body, Timeless Mind,* he agrees with an Indian teacher who said the following:

> As is the microcosm, so is the macrocosm.
> As is the atom, so is the universe.
> As is the human body, so is the cosmic body.
> As is the human mind, so is the cosmic mind.[6]

Andrew Weil has emerged as a popular personality in the alternative medicine field and, after years of obscurity, appeared on the cover of *Time* magazine in 1997. He also echoes the all-is-One perspective. In his book *Natural Health, Natural Medicine* Weil writes,

"All religions and spiritual traditions stress the importance of overcoming the illusion of separateness and experiencing unity."[7] Weil,
like Chopra, was educated in medicine and applies his philosophy
to issues of health.

Gary Zukav, who received extensive national publicity by ap-
pearing on Oprah Winfrey's television show (also like Chopra), is
another who holds the belief that all is One. In his popular book
*The Seat of the Soul* he writes, "Physical reality and the organisms
and the forms within physical reality are systems of Light within
systems of Light, and this Light is the same Light as the Light of
your soul."[8] The ancient Hindu way of saying the same thing is
"Atman is Brahman"; the individual is one with the divine.

## INWARD, UPWARD, BUT NOT OUTWARD

During a long dinner conversation I had with a senior researcher
from a large New Age think tank, we discussed the idea of this impersonal force. For fifteen years this man had been deeply im-
mersed in Eastern philosophy. He had been researching, writing
and advising on radio and television specials about New Age topics. He had been brought up in a Christian church, and he came to
me because he was considering returning to his roots. One reason
he gave for his desire was that he couldn't find a home in any of the
Eastern philosophies. He had tried them all and found that they
didn't fit what he had discovered about the universe. Above all, he
had met the top Eastern gurus and New Age advocates and was
profoundly disappointed. He described them as narcissistic.

I explained to him that the thrust of New Age philosophy is *inward* (to the divine that is within) or *upward* (to merge your identity with that of the One), but definitely not *outward* (to a distinct
world that is illusory). I asked why he would be motivated to care

deeply about distinct people and things when his philosophy regards them as illusory. He quickly agreed that if he was true to his philosophy, he would not care at all.

For this book I did extensive interviews with a woman I'll call Susan, a college professor who for many years was a strong advocate of the New Age perspective. I asked her what she would have said about love from her former viewpoint. She said she would have believed that we need to love "being" in general. This would be an abstract loving of all creation. When I asked her if this love applied to particular, distinct though illusory things, she admitted that she wouldn't have had an answer for that question. She told me that the disconnect between her idea of love and the inability to practice it even on a small level never occurred to her.

## KNOWN BY THEIR LOVE

Tal Brooke, president of the Spiritual Counterfeits Project based in Berkeley, California, spent years in India being groomed as a Western spokesman for Sai Baba, the guru of gurus in India. Sai Baba is the guru most respected by adherents to New Age spirituality. He is the one whom many other gurus visit to be blessed. Thousands go to catch even a distant glimpse of him, for there are many stories of his miracle-working powers. Tal Brooke had numerous private audiences with Sai Baba.

During his time in India, Tal also met a Christian missionary couple. He tried to use his brilliant mind and his skills in logic to convert them to Hinduism, but they put some dents in his arguments. What he noticed about them over time was that they seemed to care more for him than they did for themselves. Later he described their attitude as other-centered, or agape love. Though other Hindu disciples were gentle, Tal noticed that they lacked the quality of genuine other-centered love. Above all, after numerous private audiences with Sai Baba, Tal realized that the guru himself utterly lacked this other-centered love. Tal Brooke began to understand what Jesus meant when he said, "By this everyone will know that you are my disciples, if you have love for one another" (John 13:35 NRSV).

Jesus also said, "A new command I give you: Love one another. As I have loved you, so you must love one another" (John 13:34). This is a command that believers in Jesus are to obey, which of course implies that it is also possible to disobey. Believers in Jesus are not automatically loving. They can be disobedient to what Jesus asks of them.

The radical nature of the love required to love as Jesus loved is stunning. Jesus gave his life for those who were in rebellion against God. Such self-sacrificial agape love is the indicator that someone is a follower of Jesus. The way other people know that believers are disciples is *by* their love, *if and only if* they love one another.[9]

When those who bear the name of Christ fail to demonstrate God's love, other people are often hurt in the process and feel justified in their unbelief. Emotional pain caused by Christians becomes an obstacle to being able to even consider who Jesus is.

At a retreat with top New Age and evangelical leaders, I had the opportunity to engage in discussions about how these unbelievers might have been hurt by Christians and how they viewed Jesus in light of their experiences. After a few days, the final person to share was the wife of one of the most prominent New Age advocates. Because of what some Christians had done to her fifteen years earlier, she had not been able to say the name of Jesus Christ. Whenever she said that name, she would break down and weep uncontrollably. She thanked me and others present for freeing her to be able to

consider who Jesus is and, for the first time in fifteen years, to say
his name.

## PASSION, A MENTOR AND A PERSPECTIVE

As I travel around the United States and overseas interacting with
believers and nonbelievers, certain common themes emerge. First,
many people desire *passion;* they want to have a passionate commitment to something or someone. Second, many also desire a
*mentor* who exemplifies love and shows them a good way to live.
Third, many people crave a *perspective* that is comprehensive
enough to make sense of both their personal and public lives.

Often people do not find what they desire in the church. Many
desire passion but find in their churches coldness or lack of emotion. They desire a mentor who embodies truth and love, but they
are disillusioned by hypocrisy and lovelessness. Despite their desire for a perspective that makes sense of things, sometimes what
they encounter in church is narrow and ineffectual to answer the
questions they are asking. They desire passionate commitment,
modeling of character and an educated conscience, but they are
unable to satisfy their hunger for these things in the church.

Of course, there are plenty of exceptions to the pattern of disap-
pointment with church. Many believers are passionately committed to Jesus, have found a mentor and have gained solid answers
to the big questions. What has made the difference? *Love.* All these
transformed believers have been pulled, sometimes kicking and
screaming, out of self-centeredness and have been overwhelmed
by God's love for them. They respond by passionately desiring to
love God with their whole being. They find God's love demonstrated in what Jesus said and did for us and are motivated by his
example to reach out and love others. They seek to grow in love by

finding a mentor who can teach in theory and in practice this life of trust in God. They eventually desire to love God more with their minds and, whether in personal or public life, to "take captive every thought to make it obedient to Christ" (2 Corinthians 10:5).

The whole message of the gospel is saturated with love. By contrast, atheism (all is matter) and New Age spirituality (all is spirit) have no adequate basis to stimulate or sustain love at all.

## A CLEAR PATH

Practically speaking, love does not grow automatically. It requires following a path that is clearly marked. Love requires *commitment, character, conscience, community* and *courage*. We can summarize how love is related to each of these qualities in this way:

> Love is never sure apart from commitment.
> Love is never sane apart from conscience.
> Love is never safe apart from character.
> Love is never stimulated apart from community.
> Love is never seized apart from courage.[10]

These topics will be the subject of our study in the next five chapters. In the final chapter we will stand back and review what we have discovered. With each topic, I will contrast the biblical approach with atheistic and New Age perspectives and show how only Jesus leads down the path to love.

I do not mean any disrespect for the character of atheists, New Age devotees or followers of any other religious view. I know many kind and loving people of other religions or no religion at all. Some nonbelievers are more loving than some believers. But when atheists and New Agers are pushed to the logical conclusions of their assumptions, love is undermined. There is no ultimate reality or adequate motive to create or sustain love. My concern is to say these things in a loving way as an expression of the God I love, who himself is love (1 John 4:8, 16). I also want to point out the path of love to others even as I struggle to follow it myself. A desperate person once cried out to Jesus, "I do believe; help me overcome my unbelief!" (Mark 9:24). I would say, "I do love; help me overcome my lack of love!"

While others have stressed love's practical value in attracting people to consider Jesus, they have not sufficiently contrasted how Christianity, atheism and pantheism differ in their ability to give a real foundation for agape love. Although we could also make the case that agape love is more central and pervasive in Christianity than in any other religious perspective, including Judaism and Islam, we can only take time here to focus on materialism and pantheism.

Another unique contribution of faith in Christ is that the path to love involves the five areas outlined above: *commitment, conscience, character, community* and *courage*. Faith in Christ supports and sustains all five, while atheism and pantheism in the end undermine them all. Not only is the concept of love subverted, but the necessary components of motivating and upholding love over time are compromised.

My purpose is also to inspire those who bear the name of Christ to be truer examples of Christ's love. I heard a story about Alexander the Great that illustrates this point. One day the great Greek conqueror was holding court when a young man who was guilty of cowardice in battle—something Alexander despised—was brought to him. From high on his throne Alexander asked, "What is your name?" The young man, knowing that Alexander held the power of life and death, was shaking and could barely speak. He answered in a trembling voice, "Alexander." Alexander the Great stood up from his throne and asked again, "What is your name?" The young man responded in an even shakier voice, "Alexander." Alexander the Great stepped down from his throne and shouted, *"What is your name?"* By this time the man could hardly speak and responded in a barely audible voice, "Alexander." Alexander the Great shouted, "Change your conduct or change your name!" We, too, must take the name of Christ with courage and care.[11]

Further, I want to stress the uniqueness of Christ's love in both theory and practice. Sometimes his love is expressed in words, as in the example of the missionary couple who befriended Tal Brooke. Sometimes it is a silent love. I recently heard of a tribe in Nigeria that approached a missionary who didn't know them. The chief said, "We all want to believe in Jesus. What do we do?" The missionary was confused and asked if someone had preached to them. They said no but again stated that the whole tribe wanted to follow Jesus. When the missionary asked why, the chief explained. Apparently some Christian believers had been coming to their village regularly over a number of years and had built a school, some wells, a hospital and other things to help them. The villagers said that no one else had done anything for them. They were attracted to the loving attitudes and actions of these believers. There is spoken love and silent love. One or the other may be needed at different times.[12]

## DOES OUR WORLDVIEW FIT THE WORLD?

*As John winds down his remarks, Annette says, "Isn't that what we were talking about before? People who aren't Christians often show more love than so-called Christians."*

*"That's true sometimes," John admits, "but if Christians fail to love,*

it isn't because they're Christians. It's because they have not lived up to their own view of life. And non-Christians who act lovingly actually have not lived down to their view of life."

Simon has been fidgeting in his chair for several minutes. Now he says, "Okay, you've made your case that love is somehow logically inconsistent with atheism. So what? Does love have to be tied to logic? I can choose to love other people anyway, can't I?"

Mike says, "Sure you can, but at least you acknowledge that you're inconsistent."

For a moment John struggles with how to respond. Then he says, "All I'm saying is that there's a basis for love in Jesus Christ and the message of the gospel that you won't find anywhere else."

"Which would be great," Simon replies, "if any of it were true."

For a while the group appears to retreat into their own thoughts. Then Julia says, "John, what you're saying about Christians and love—it's beautiful. But Christians aren't the only ones who believe in love. I mean, I'm not a Christian, but love is very important to me. It's like _____ says. (She names a well-known New Age author.) We talk about individuals and personalities and all, but that's just an illusion. It's really all energy anyway. All love. We're all part of the whole, part of each other. So we're all part of God, and we generate our own love."

Simon asks, "If everybody distinct from you is an illusion, who is there to love?"

Mike suggests, "Maybe you don't believe other people are distinct entities, but you have to act like it."

Annette, who has been quiet for a while, says, "Well, you can't go around ignoring everybody like they aren't really there."

John says, "One of the marks of truth is that it fits what we believe about the real world. What if we believe love is important, but our worldview has no basis for love? Then we have to either question our view of the world or question the importance of love."

Simon becomes more intense. "Maybe we need to be brave enough to face the fact that there is no real basis for love. Maybe love gives you a purpose in life, but somebody else finds purpose some other way."

"Love does give you purpose," Annette says with great intensity. "Love is the purpose."

John checks the time and says with some regret, "We have to wrap it up for tonight, but I hope to see everybody back here next week. Let me give you a preview of what we'll be considering in the rest of our studies. We'll look at how followers of Christ see love and learn to practice it—if they're being consistent, that is," he adds, looking at Julia. "And we'll explore the ways some other belief systems try to answer some basic questions about love."

Mike quips, "Like how to find it?"

They all laugh. John nods. "Well, that one's pretty basic. But I was thinking of some other questions. Maybe you'd like to jot them down now so you can be thinking about them during the week." He reads aloud from his notes:

"How do you place a high value on the personal if the universe is impersonal?

"How can you be committed to justice or human rights if there is no objective good or evil?

"How can you inform character and conscience if everything is relative?

"How can you forge lasting community if there is no necessity to forgive and no sin to be forgiven?

"How can you be courageous if there are no adequate reasons to do so and no basis for hope in the future?"

# LOVE AND COMMITMENT

## Love Is Never Sure
## Apart from Commitment

*As the study group convenes in the bookstore coffee shop, John watches their faces closely. Was anyone offended by last week's discussion? He is relieved to find a warm friendliness and banter as they all get their drinks and snacks and sit down. They scoot their chairs in close to the table and exchange good and bad snippets of the past week—car problems, a letter from a long-lost classmate, a computer glitch solved. John smiles and thinks,* We come from different backgrounds and hold different views, but we can talk about them freely and accept each other. We're experiencing love right here, at least the friendship type.

*John begins the discussion. "Tonight we're going to explore the idea* love is never sure apart from commitment. *We'll look at the teaching of Jesus in a portion of Scripture, Mark 8:34-38."*

*Annette looks suspicious. "What do you mean, love is never sure apart from commitment?"*

*"I mean that even if a loving relationship starts out, it can't be continued, sustained or nurtured without commitment."*

*"Well, my boyfriend and I are committed to each other," Annette responds.*

*John wonders if there is a little uncertainty in her voice. He says,*
"Most people have a yearning to be deeply committed to someone or
something. So we're going to look at what Jesus said about commitment. And we'll ask whether atheism or New Age spirituality can provide a sufficient foundation for commitment."

*Lightly, but with an edge to his voice, Simon responds,* "So now
you're telling me that I can't make commitments because I don't believe
in God."

*John answers,* "Well, many atheists are very committed to their
atheism. Or they're really passionate about political causes. But it
seems to me that a big part of atheism is autonomy."

*Simon looks puzzled.* "And by autonomy you mean . . ."

"That we are not accountable to anyone or to any moral values outside whatever personal code we decide on for ourselves. Nothing in
atheism requires us to commit ourselves to anything. If there is no God,
in fact, there is nothing worth committing ourselves to, nothing we
would call most worthy."

*Simon starts to speak, but Julia interrupts.* "Maybe that's true of
atheists, but lots of people who follow New Age spirituality are committed to causes like the environment and holistic health and peace
and justice."

"That's certainly true and commendable," *John says,* "but why do
they feel so committed? If you hold to the all-is-One principle, why
would you want to change anything? It seems to me that you'd have to
either give up your philosophy or give up your causes."

*Julia protests,* "But if everything is divine, if it's all part of God, then
of course we should honor the earth and try to save the planet. And—"

*Mike speaks up.* "I want to say something about commitment. It
seems to me that younger people don't understand commitment. At
least not long-term commitment." *His voice rises.* "They change jobs,

*change churches, change spouses, change . . . well, I won't even say what all they change. What ever happened to consistency?"*

*Everybody (except John) starts talking at once. Julia says something about her former husband. Simon says something about his former boss. Annette says something about* Leave It to Beaver. *Mike says something about patriotism. People at other tables glance over at the group and look away.*

*John holds up both hands. "Hold on. I think at least we all agree we would like to commit ourselves to something worthy." As everyone quiets down, he says, "Let's talk about that idea, and perhaps we can shed some light on our questions."*

## COMMITTED TO A CAUSE

Like members of John's study group, many people take commitment for granted. They are not aware that other worldviews fail to motivate or sustain commitment, and that commitment and love are inseparable. Jim Elliot and Nate Saint were two Christian missionaries who became martyrs trying to take the gospel to the Auca Indians in South America. Their story is portrayed in the film *End of the Spear*. They and their fellow missionaries were committed to the eternal and temporal good of these people. They were even willing to give their lives if necessary. Jim Elliot wrote, "He is no fool who gives what he cannot keep to gain what he cannot lose." Amazingly, the families of these martyrs not only forgave the murderers but chose to live with them and help them in every way. Years later Steve Saint, Nate Saint's son, came to be baptized by the same man who had murdered his father. They traveled around, speaking of the reconciliation and forgiveness of Christ.

William Wilberforce, whose life is portrayed in the film *Amazing Grace,* was a deeply committed believer in Christ and a member of the British parliament from 1784 to 1812. His commitment led him to his great cause, the abolition of slavery. It took more than thirty years for him to see the accomplishment of his goal. Christian theologian and minister John Wesley wrote to Wilberforce that unless God had raised him up for this cause, he would be overwhelmed by the opposition he would face. Because of his faith in Christ, Wilberforce was able to fight against injustice and oppression. He loved his neighbor—the slaves—as he loved himself, because he loved God.

Gary Haugen, president of International Justice Mission, says that there are more slaves today than in Wilberforce's day. Haugen and his staff of three hundred are committed, because of their faith in Christ, to bringing slave holders to justice, freeing slaves, working for structural social change to prevent more abuse, and becoming involved with victim aftercare. Both of these antislavery movements were begun by Christians who were moved by oppression to commit themselves to a worthy cause.

*There is within people a deep yearning to commit to that which is most worthy.* People will protest for or against a war. They will become public advocates for or against immigration policies, abortion or same-sex marriage. Many are passionate about personal or public causes. They believe that their views are right. Yet in light of widespread relativism, when two-thirds of people (in the United States) believe that there is no absolute right or wrong, it is surprising that people can be so sure of their positions. How can they speak about justice or injustice, right or wrong, when they say they don't believe in any such thing? In practice, or at least in words, relativists act as if there are objective values, while in theory they deny them.

## SUFFICIENT REASON WHY

In his classic study *Habits of the Heart,* sociologist Robert Bellah of the University of California at Berkeley had his team interview people throughout the United States concerning their commitment to friendship, marriage, community life and political life. Bellah's striking conclusion was that although many people in our North American society considered themselves committed to other people and community and political life, they had great difficulty articulating *why* they were committed, except for their own selfish benefit. His book is a haunting one that deserves our attention. If we are to be committed to someone or something outside ourselves, is there a sufficient reason why?[1]

In his inaugural address, President John F. Kennedy said, "Ask not what your country can do for you—ask what you can do for your country." The statement resonates with many people as true and profound, but *why* is it true and profound? If we are accountable only to ourselves, why should we do things for others if it is not to our own immediate benefit?

We could restate the concept any number of ways: "Ask not what your spouse can do for you; ask what you can do for your spouse." "Ask not what another can do for you; ask what you can do for another." The call is similar to Jesus' teaching that is known as the Golden Rule: "In everything, do to others what you would have them do to you" (Matthew 7:12). Where can we find a motivation for this other-centered, committed love? Certainly not in atheism or New Age spirituality.

It is difficult to see how atheism or New Age spirituality gives us any basis to judge or hope for anything as *most worthy,* or gives us something worthy of our passion, or gives us any clear guidelines for living. Unless there is something of real value, something most worthy, then commitment as well as love are undermined.

## IMPLICATIONS OF UNBELIEF

Leading postmodern philosopher Jacques Derrida grasps the implications of unbelief. His philosophy is opposed to *logocentrism,* the idea that there is any meaning or purpose to life. He doesn't believe that there is any "transcendent signifier" or infinite reference point (as Sartre called it) or any sense to the world coming from outside the world (as Wittgenstein called it). For Derrida, there is no fixed point by which we can judge what is right or wrong, just or unjust. Yet—inconsistently—he maintains that the reason for deconstructing texts is that "deconstruction is justice." But we can know what is just only if we have a fixed and transcendent standard to identify it. Derrida is committed to uncovering injustice, but he has no basis in his philosophy to define justice. He wants commitment but denies any ultimate basis for commitment.

Another postmodern philosopher, Richard Rorty, gives up on belief in God and comes to the conclusion that there is "no neutral ground" by which we can judge that the Holocaust was evil.[2] He maintains that the basis for ethics is "sentiment."[3] But what makes one person's sentiment—say, that of a Nazi or a terrorist—better than another person's sentiment? In Rorty's system, there is no objective way to make that judgment. I don't think he would be against pragmatic commitment to many diverse causes, but I think he would oppose the idea that any cause was intrinsically or objectively better than any other.

Forms of New Age spirituality rooted in the Theravada or Buddhist tradition discourage passionate commitment to anything.

Desire is the source of all our problems. We want money, power, sex or relationship, but when we don't get what we want, we experience pain and sorrow. The Buddhist answer is to cure the headache of desire by decapitation—to eliminate it. *Nirvana* in Sanskrit means "to extinguish" or "to blow out," as in blowing out a flame. The flame of desire must be blown out. Thus it would not be appropriate to be passionately committed to any cause. A person should not be unduly attached to anything.

Jesus does not want to extinguish desire but to purify it and then raise it to the highest possible degree. We are to seek first God's kingdom (Matthew 6:33). We are to passionately hunger and thirst for righteousness, and we will be satisfied (Matthew 5:6). Jesus himself showed passion. He wept over Jerusalem (Luke 19:41) and at the grave of his friend Lazarus (John 11:35). He experienced great joy after the successful ministry of seventy of his disciples (Luke 10:21). Jesus was angry when the religious leaders wanted to prevent him from healing on the Sabbath (Mark 3:5). Jesus was a man of deep passion, and he encourages such passion in his followers.

According to Hindu philosopher Shankara, there seems to be no basis for valuing human dignity or human rights. He says, "Who are you? Who am I? Whence have I come? Who is my mother? Who is my father—think of all of this as having no substance, leave it all as the stuff of dreams."[4]

Os Guinness elaborates further in his book *Unspeakable: Facing Up to Evil in an Age of Genocide and Terror:*

> This view of ultimate reality means that neither traditional Hinduism nor traditional Buddhism shows the slightest concern about human rights. . . . Entirely logical within their own frames of thinking, Hinduism and Buddhism regard the

Western passion for human rights as a form of narcissism as well as delusion. R. C. Zaehner, who followed Radakrishnan in the Spaulding Chair of Eastern Religions and Ethics at Oxford University, underscored their logic bluntly: "In practice it means that neither religion in its classical formulation pays the slightest attention to what goes on in the world today."[5]

Such a world-denying quality makes it impossible to consistently address social issues.

Others in New Age spirituality value passion, but it is difficult to see what they can be passionately committed to. If there is nothing distinct from ourselves, how can we be committed to it? Passionate practices could lead to altered states of consciousness, but their purpose would be to take you out of this illusory world rather than to incline you toward commitment to anything or anyone in it.

When Susan, the ex-New Age college professor, would experience problems in a relationship, her response was to never remain committed but to leave the relationship because it was causing a spiritual disruption. She believed that if you had a problem, you changed your choice and created a new reality. Most of her friends during that time in her life were single or divorced. None of her friends really believed that it was wrong to leave a spouse. Constantly picking and choosing different pieces of ideologies allowed her to live any kind of life she wanted to live. She could do whatever she wanted to do. But she didn't really see that in this way she could not pursue a sustained, committed relationship.

Many in New Age and Neo-Pagan spirituality are committed to the environment. But if you believe the world to be nondistinct and illusory, why should you be concerned about separate species, trees or plants? New Age author George Leonard says in his book

*The Transformation* that one Western myth that needs to be ques-
tioned and set aside by those pursuing Eastern philosophy is the
"myth of the separate species." He says that there is only one species on this planet, and that is life on earth. He also questions the
"myth of the separate ego." When people recover the Eastern way
of thinking, Leonard says, they will do away with Western psychology's obsession with our own ego and realize that "consciousness has no skin."[6]

If we are to take the principle of nondistinction seriously, then
how can we be concerned about separate trees in the Brazilian rain
forest? How can it be important to fight for the preservation of distinct species like the humpback whale, the cheetah or the snail
darter? New Age philosophy pulls the rug out from under the very
positions its adherents so passionately proclaim.

## CARING FOR CREATION

On the other hand, there is a strong biblical basis for caring for the
environment.[7] Genesis 1:26-28 provides what some call the Cultural Mandate because in these verses God calls humanity, both
male and female, to exercise dominion or rulership over the whole
creation—fish, birds, livestock and every other living creature.
Some in New Age spirituality claim that this passage has given
Christians the excuse to rape and pillage the earth. Certainly we
can point to believers who have abused the earth. But to see that
this is not what the biblical mandate means, we need only read a
little further, to Genesis 2:15: "The LORD God took the man and
put him in the Garden of Eden to work it and take care of it."

First, it appears from this passage that the man was made for the
Garden rather than the Garden being made for the man. Second,
the words translated "work" and "take care of" emphasize the im-

portance of serving and caring for the creation rather than destroy-
ing it. In any case, I want to stress that some of the things people
in New Age spirituality are committed to, such as environmental-
ism, are undermined by their own worldview, but that there is a
biblical basis for upholding these same concerns.

Both atheists and New Age practitioners are passionately committed to many issues. But if all is matter or all is somehow illusory,
how can you judge anything as more worthy than another thing
except by personal or corporate preference? This contradiction
will appear repeatedly throughout our study. G. K. Chesterton, in
his book *Orthodoxy,* points out how philosophies often undermine
themselves by asserting contradictory ideas:

> All denunciation implies a moral doctrine of some kind and
> the modern skeptic doubts not only the institution he de-
> nounces, but the doctrine by which he denounces it. Thus he
> writes one book complaining that imperial oppression insults
> the purity of women, and then writes another book, a novel
> in which he insults it himself. As a politician, he will cry out
> that war is a waste of life, and then as a philosopher that all
> of life is a waste of time. A Russian pessimist will denounce a
> policeman for killing a peasant, and then prove by the highest
> philosophical principles that the peasant ought to have killed
> himself. A man denounces marriage as a lie and then de-
> nounces aristocratic profligates for treating it as a lie.
>
> A man of this school goes first to a political meeting where
> he complains that the savages are treated as if they are beasts.
> Then he takes his hat and umbrella and goes to a scientific
> meeting where he proves that they practically are beasts. In
> short, the modern revolutionist, being an infinite skeptic, is

forever engaged in undermining his own mines. In his book on politics, he attacks men for trampling on morality; in his book on ethics, he attacks morality for trampling on men. Therefore, the modern man in revolt becomes practically useless for all purposes of revolt. By rebelling against everything, he has lost his right to rebel against anything.[8]

## SWITCHING THE PRICE TAGS

Whether we like it or not, we are constantly making commitments. Some things rise toward a position of ultimate concern while others fall to a lesser place.

It is said that some thieves once broke into a store. They did not steal anything, but they did switch the price tags. An eight-hundred-dollar television was priced at twenty dollars, some imitation jewelry became five hundred dollars, and so on throughout the store. The next day people paid those mistaken prices.

In the same way, people switch the price tags on the things they value. Petty things assume enormous importance while genuinely important things receive little attention. There is a continuing need to switch back the price tags so that first things are first, second things second, third things third and so on.

## PLACING A TRUE VALUE ON EVERYTHING

Jonathan Edwards, considered by some Americans to have been our greatest philosopher and theologian, argued in his book *The Nature of True Virtue* that true virtue is placing a true value on everything.[9] It's not enough to *say* what our priorities are; we must actually *live* that way. Some believers in Christ use the acronym JOY—Jesus Christ, Others, You—to indicate the priorities we ought to have.

Edwards argued that virtue is a matter of proportion. It's not enough to place first things first; we must ask how much they *deserve* to be first. It's not enough to place second things second. We need to proportion our commitment to the degree each concern deserves. If Jesus is first, how weighty is our commitment to him compared to our other commitments? Where does our family rank, and to what degree does that commitment deserve our attention?

## COMMITTED TO LASTING LOVE

Love is never motivated or sustained or fulfilled without a conscious commitment to do so. Love for a friend will not continue without commitment. Love for a spouse will not last apart from commitment. A community will never last unless its members are committed to it.

The things we love most passionately shape the way we live and the kind of person we become. Puritan writer Henry Scougal said, "The worth of a soul is determined by the object of its loves." A life passionately lived for that which is most worthy is the fullest kind of life possible. Fullness of life comes not through the number of our years but through the quality of that which we love. An anonymous poem says:

> We live in deeds, not years
> In thoughts, not breaths
> In feelings, not in figures on a dial.
> He lives most who thinks most, feels most nobly, and acts
>    the best.

## THE ONE OF INFINITE WORTH

If we seek to love that which is highest, we must look to the One who is of infinite worth, feel passionately about him and his cause, and act faithfully. People differ on what is worthy or not worthy. If there is an infinite, personal God who created us and redeemed us, then he deserves our allegiance. We are not our own; we are bought with a price (1 Corinthians 6:19-20). It is he whom we are to love with mind, heart, soul and strength (Mark 12:30). We are called to renew our minds (Romans 12:2), hunger and thirst for righteousness (Matthew 5:6) and obey what Christ commands because we love him (John 14:15). We are called to think, feel and act for him. It is because he loved us that we are to love others. Such radical love is not sustained without a conscious commitment.

We can see how commitment sustains love in a marriage relationship. All marriages have difficulties. The degree of commitment determines the longevity of the marriage. Ruth Graham (Billy Graham's wife) was asked if she had ever contemplated divorce. Her answer was, "Divorce? No. Murder? Yes."[10]

At the altar we make a promise to love, but what enables us to sustain that promise through times of strain? The answer is commitment. I have often said that my confidence in my wife's love is not rooted in her relationship to me but in her relationship to Christ. At times my only hope is that she loves Christ more than she loves me, and Christ loves me more than she does at that time. A passionate love for our Lord is a precondition for sustaining our love for our spouses, friends or neighbors.

The apostle Paul wrote that people have a tendency to worship and serve created things rather than the Creator (Romans 1:25). Whenever we take something or someone in God's creation and make it an object of *ultimate* concern, we give that person or thing the place that only God should have. We *worth-ship* it, and it becomes an idol. Material things, money, sex and power often dominate people's values, but other more innocuous concerns can also usurp God's place in worship. For example, we can pursue the god of self-image, attempting to feel good about ourselves even as we pursue ungodly patterns of living. When our strategy fails, we may turn to drugs, alcohol or sex in a quest to feel better about ourselves.

Another commonly worshiped idol is the god of conformity. It is easy to be afraid of being different, out of the mainstream or not in accordance with the mood of the community, nation or age in which we live. In Washington, D.C., the dominant value is power. In Hollywood, it is fame. On New York's Wall Street, money rules. In other areas, complacency, relativism and indiscriminate tolerance are dominant forces. To go against the reigning value in any area is to risk rejection. Some people pursue the god of affect, attempting to feel great all the time and becoming disappointed when they feel low. Again they may turn to artificial means such as drugs, alcohol or other addictions in an attempt to attain the high they do not feel otherwise. Another god people worship is the extraordinary. This idol makes them easily bored by the ordinariness of life, but heroism in significant moments is forged in the small, everyday choices we make.

Widespread relativism in our culture undermines clarity about what truly deserves our commitment. We are unsure of what, if anything, is most worthy. It is difficult, if not impossible, to sustain loving relationships without a clear idea of what we are committing to and why we are doing it. Without commitment, love becomes unsure. To the degree that we dispense with fixed moral norms, our personal, corporate and national commitments become hesitant and tentative.

Recovering our commitment to our Lord involves not only regaining a vision of the truth about God but also a sense of his goodness and beauty. When we grasp the winsome attractiveness of God, then we can rekindle a white-hot passion for the incomparable beauty of our Lord.

## PICK UP YOUR CROSS

When you are faced with doing something that you know to be right but is still difficult, the cost will always be too high—unless you have a sufficient reason *why* you ought to do it. If you do not know why you want to get in shape, exercising will be too painful. If you do not know why you want to lose weight, saying no to food will be too difficult. In order to carry through on any commitment, we must have a sufficient reason why. The *why* must be sufficiently motivating to sustain our commitment. It is not enough to have a reason; the reason must be compelling.

Jesus does not merely command commitment; he gives us compelling reasons why we ought to act accordingly. Jesus said, "If any want to become my followers, let them deny themselves and take up their cross and follow me" (Mark 8:34 NRSV). If you claim to be a disciple or a follower of Christ, then he requires self-denial, saying no to yourself. The self-denial that Christ requires does not mean saying no to being a distinct, individual person—a *self*—as New Age spirituality demands. Christ's self-denial does not mean saying no to the *"new self"* that is created in the image of Christ (Colossians 3:10). The self-denial of Christ means saying no to our sinful desires—what the Bible sometimes calls the *old self.*

William Barclay explained self-denial as enthronement of God in place of self:

To deny oneself means in every moment of life to say "no" to self and "yes" to God. To deny oneself means once and for all to dethrone self and to enthrone God. To deny oneself means to obliterate self as the dominant principle of life and to make God the ruling principle, more, the ruling passion of life. The life of constant self-*denial* is a life of constant assent to God.[11]

The word for *deny* in the Greek text of the New Testament (Mark 8:34) is *aparneomai,* which means "completely disown." It is the same word used with respect to Peter's denials of Christ (Matthew 26:34, 70, 72, 74). Pastor John MacArthur draws this comparison:

> That's exactly the kind of denial a believer is to make in regard to *himself.* He has either to disown himself or refuse to acknowledge the self of the old man. Jesus' words could be paraphrased. "Let him refuse to have any association or companionship with himself. Self-denial not only characterizes a person when he comes in saving faith to Christ but also as he lives as a faithful disciple of Christ."[12]

The metaphor that Christ uses next makes the difficulty even more overwhelming. We are called to pick up our cross. The cross is a familiar symbol to us. As you drive through any major city, look for how many times you see the shape of the cross on churches. Sometimes the cross is a mere ornament worn on a necklace. But the cross in Jesus' day meant something very different: an agonizing form of execution that the Romans used exclusively for foreigners.

Jesus' command to take up your cross would have shocked his hearers. Today it would be as if he said, "Unless you pick up your electric chair or carry the rifle to be used in your firing squad or carry the noose to be used at your hanging, you cannot be my disciple." Death on a cross was excruciating (a word drawn from the Latin word for *crucifixion*).

The Romans reserved the cross as a form of punishment for those in foreign-occupied territories. Cicero said that the cross should not even be named by a Roman citizen. It was a graphic deterrent to rebellion against Rome.

Not many years before Jesus came to Caesarea Philippi, where he said these words about taking up your cross, one hundred men were crucified in that very area. Before that, around 100 B.C., eight hundred Jewish rebels were crucified in Jerusalem. After the revolt following the death of Herod the Great, two thousand were crucified under the Roman proconsul Varas. There were many crucifixions on a smaller scale. Some estimate that during the lifetime of Christ, there were thirty thousand crucifixions under Roman authority. So "to take up your cross" meant "to be willing to start on a death march . . . to be willing to suffer the indignities, the pain and even the death of a condemned criminal."[13]

## SAVING BY LOSING

Knowing all this, why would anyone choose to answer Jesus when he calls, "Follow me"? Jesus gives a sufficient reason why we ought to say no to self and endure the cross. He says, "Those who want to save their life will lose it, and those who lose their life for my sake, and for the sake of the gospel, will save it" (Mark 8:35 NRSV).

If you try to be your own savior, to pursue your own pleasure and do things your own way, to pursue any of the false gods mentioned earlier, then you will lose your life. Not only will you lose your life eternally, but you will lose the satisfaction of life here and now. From Jesus' teaching, we are aware of the specter of eternal judgment that hangs over us; but we are less aware that choosing the way of self-salvation means losing life's fullness in the present.

John Piper argues that "God is most glorified in me when I am most satisfied in Him."[14] God's glory and our own self-satisfaction meet in exactly the same place. Following God's glory is the way to eternal joy and present joy. You might argue (along with Augustine, Pascal, Jonathan Edwards, C. S. Lewis and others) that all sin is exchanging a higher satisfaction for a lesser one. For instance, pride is saying no to God's joy in order to say yes to taking pleasure in yourself. Covetousness is saying no to God's joy in order to take pleasure in acquiring material things. Certainly there is pleasure to be found in pursuing lesser things, but sooner or later the pleasure fades and then is lost. My favorite quote from C. S. Lewis is this:

> Our Lord finds our desires not too strong, but too weak. We are half-hearted creatures fooling about with drink, sex, and ambition when infinite joy is offered us, like an ignorant child, who wants to go on making mud pies in a slum because he cannot imagine what is meant by the offer of a holiday at the sea. We are far too easily pleased.[15]

We do not even desire our own greatest happiness. Giving your all for secondary things such as alcohol, sex and ambition is saying no to infinite joy. On the other hand, by saying yes to first things like the infinite joy offered us, we can rightly enjoy secondary things in the way God intends.

## THE SELF-INTEREST OF SELF-DENIAL

Pursuing your own selfish ways may lead to pleasure; but with the law of diminishing returns, it ultimately leads to despair, decay and addiction. On the other hand, if you lose your life for the sake of

Christ and the gospel, you will save your life eternally and gain abundant life now.

Self-denial turns out to be in our self-interest. But self-interest is not the same as selfishness. The central choice is for Christ and the gospel; we benefit only as a side effect. We are lost in wonder, awe and praise as we behold Christ, yet we are assuredly happy.

We are perhaps most joyful when we are unselfconscious. It is not selfish to behold the Grand Canyon and experience awe. It is not selfish to enjoy a valued friend and lose yourself in conversation with that person, yet still be filled with joy. You are not being selfish or self-oriented, yet these experiences are in your self-interest.

Jesus said, "I have come that they may have life, and have it to the full" (John 10:10). Faith in Christ is not opposed to *life* but to *sin*. Faith in Christ is not opposed to the creation but to the Fall of humanity. Our faith is life-affirming and creation-enjoying. Following Christ is the way to the fullness of life, while rejecting Christ is the way to losing out on life in all its fullness.

All sin is life-taking in the sense that it drains life from us. To be sure, some Christians are so focused on the Fall or on the possibility of sin that they come across as negative toward life and creation. But we can have faith that is life-affirming and creation-enjoying without minimizing the Fall or the danger of sin.

## THE BEST INVESTMENT

After Jesus said that people must lose their lives for his sake in order to save their lives, Jesus went on to ask, "What will it profit them to gain the whole world and forfeit their life? Indeed, what can they give in return for their life?" (Mark 8:36-37 NRSV). Jesus calls us to weigh our values. What kind of investment do you want to make? What if you gain everything—money, fame, power, sex—

and lose your soul? Who would make that kind of investment? It is better to give up everything temporal—time, money, even life on this earth—in exchange for that which is eternal and has infinite value and cannot be lost.

Choosing otherwise would be foolish, yet people make that choice all the time. They constantly find that the things they desire are not adequate to satisfy them. So they get a new car, a new house, a new vacation spot or a new spouse. Sooner or later the newness wears off, and they continue from thing to thing, person to person, always seeking but never finding ultimate satisfaction. They want more from life but do not know where to find it. C. S. Lewis expressed the dilemma—and the way out of it:

> This principle runs through all life from top to bottom. Give up yourself and you will find your real self. Lose your life and you will save it. Submit to death, death of your ambitions and favorite wishes every day and the death of your whole body in the end; submit with every fiber of your being, and you will find eternal life. Keep back nothing. Nothing that you have not given away will ever be yours. Nothing in you that has not died will ever be raised from the dead. Look for yourself, and you will find in the long run only hatred, loneliness, despair, rage, ruin, and decay. But look for Christ and you will find Him, and with Him everything else thrown in.[16]

## NO NEED TO BE ASHAMED

Jesus concluded his call to commitment by saying, "Those who are ashamed of me and of my words in this adulterous and sinful generation, of them the Son of Man will also be ashamed when he comes in the glory of his Father with the holy angels" (Mark 8:38

NRSV). There is no need to be ashamed of the gospel; it is the "power of God for the salvation of everyone who believes" (Romans 1:16). God is not ashamed to be called our God (Hebrews 11:16), so how can we be ashamed to be identified with him?

We do not need to be ashamed of the gospel intellectually. It is hard for the heart to passionately embrace what the mind doubts, but Christianity has an advantage. Many of the foremost thinkers of all time have been believers. The best minds the world has known—people such as the apostle Paul, Augustine, John Calvin, Jonathan Edwards and C. S. Lewis—have given in-depth answers to all the classic objections to Christianity. The Lord has given us enough of the top minds that we might not despair, but not so many that we might presume. Our goal is not to gain intellectual respectability but to find out what is true. The cross is still a stumbling block to the pride of intellectuals; humbling themselves is the hardest thing for many of them to do.

Many more believers need to be made aware of the solid intellectual foundations of their faith. Some are in a state of doubt, fearing that the next question might mean an end to their faith. Many half-baked arguments are floating around and are used by nonbelievers to confuse believers. Although apologetics cannot provide absolute certainty, it can make our commitment a leap into the direction revealed by the light rather than a leap into the dark.

While there is plenty of evidence to make a commitment beyond a reasonable doubt, only God's Holy Spirit can give us absolute certainty. Anything worth believing wholeheartedly can also be doubted. Even if you establish a strong intellectual framework for your faith, it will not immunize you against doubt. What matters is how you deal with doubts, whether your own or those of others. It is said that at age sixteen, atheist Bertrand Russell asked some hard questions and was told, "Don't doubt, just believe." That was the end of his professed faith. Intellectual doubts and questions need to be faced and given clear answers. If you do not know the answer, that's OK—but find someone who does.[17]

Relativism can be an obstacle to commitment. If whatever is true for you is true for you, and whatever is true for me is true for me, then everybody is right. But then in fact nobody is right. There is still what Francis Schaeffer called "true truth," truth that is true, independent of anyone's attitude toward it. Relativism leads to halfhearted commitment. Why should I be passionately committed to what is only my private view? Why should I give my whole life in the way Christ asks if this is only my community's perspective? Unless we are unequivocal on the issue of truth, it will not be clear who or what we are calling people to be committed to.

## COMMITMENT DISTORTED

It is true that the commitment Christ calls us to make can be distorted into fanaticism. The Bible commends some kinds of zeal, but not all. There is zeal that is "not based on knowledge" (Romans 10:2). Cults issue a call to zeal and commitment and use it to strip their recruits of time, money, previous relationships, family and identity. Some may even use the same language of commitment to Christ, but it is twisted to mean total submission to cult leaders' authority and utter willingness to give up themselves for the goals of the group. The Bible does not encourage this kind of authoritarianism.

An argument against abuse is not an argument against right use. Faith in Christ does not require isolation from family and friends, stonewalling questions, hostility toward groups with a different viewpoint or the crushing of individual personality. Commitment to Christ encourages relationships with family, demonstrates the willingness to acknowledge truth wherever it is found and cultivates honesty about what commitment means. It is important to note that fanatical zeal without knowledge should not prevent zeal in accordance with knowledge.[18]

## WHAT CAN WE DO?

We can commit ourselves to the Lord. Even after becoming believers, we need to regularly restore our commitment. The glorified Christ called the Ephesian church to repent and recapture their first love (Revelation 2:4-5). We Christians need to go back to where we once were, confess our sin and refocus on Jesus.

In a marriage ceremony, a great commitment is made. An Anglican prayer book uses these words:

With my body I thee worship
With all my worldly goods I thee endow
For richer or for poorer
For better or worse
In sickness or in health
Till death do us part.

The marriage partners give their bodies and their worldly goods to each other. There is nothing else left for them to give. The terms of the commitment are for better or for worse, although neither knows what the other will be like in five, ten, twenty or fifty years. They pledge themselves to each other for richer or for poorer, not knowing what their financial position will be. They commit themselves to each other in both sickness and health, not knowing what physical illnesses they may have to face together. Many men and women are eager to make such a total commitment to another human being. But how many have made that kind of commitment to our Lord?

What if we said these words to him?

Lord, with my body I thee worship
With all my worldly goods I thee endow
For better or worse
For richer or poorer
In sickness or in health
I offer my body as a living sacrifice to you
You alone are worthy to receive my worship
You are the One before whom the angels bow and say, "Holy, holy, holy is the LORD Almighty; the whole earth is full of his glory." (Isaiah 6:3)

You are the one before whom the elders fall down and say, "Worthy is the Lamb, who was slain, to receive power and wealth and wisdom and strength and honor and glory and praise!" (Revelation 5:12)

## GODLY LEADERSHIP

Because believers too often lack such total commitment to Christ, they also lack strong, godly leadership in the church. You can't accomplish a great goal unless you are totally committed to it.

I once heard a story about Bill Pannell, who now teaches at Fuller Theological Seminary. In the 1970s he was talking to fellow African American students who were contemplating a violent revolution. One of them asked Bill, "When's the revolution going to be?"

Bill said, "There's not going to be any revolution."

They asked, "Why not?"

Bill replied, "Because of the weekend."[19]

I had to think about that story for a while before I understood the point. For five days a week, the students were into their cause. But when Friday and Saturday night came, they went out and partied. They got so wiped out on the weekend that it took until Wednesday to get the "revolution" going again. When we take "weekends" from our faith, we lose our momentum and it's difficult to get up to speed again.

## WE NEED A PUSH

I recently watched the Tour de France and noticed that at the beginning of the individual time trials, the competitors began on a downward ramp to get up to speed quickly. When riders fell during the race, often someone would help them up and give them a push to get going again. Similarly, when our spiritual momentum has stopped, we need a boost. Ultimately the Holy Spirit's help is what we need most, but it doesn't hurt to have brothers and sisters praying for us and pushing us to get going again.

We need to judge what is most worthy—our Lord—and passionately commit ourselves to him again and again. We need to say no to selfishness and say yes to our own best interests and the One who alone is worthy of worship. We need to ask not what our Lord can do for us, but what we can do for our Lord. There are many issues that we have to face in this nation and in our world, and we need passionately committed believers who have the courage to follow the divine call and use God-given gifts to build up the kingdom and love people in the name of Christ. Rick Warren, author of *The Purpose Driven Life* and pastor of Saddleback Church, was asked if he was afraid of failure in his new quest to solve the problem of AIDS in Africa. He said no. He wants his tombstone to read "At Least He Tried."

## SUMMARY

We have a deep yearning to be committed to something worthy.

Unless we are committed, love will not be sustained, either in personal or public life.

Atheism and pantheism have no adequate basis to judge meaning, purpose or moral values that would show us where we ought to commit our lives or what we ought to love. Believers need to "switch the price tags" on their commitments so that first things are really first.

Jesus calls us to radical commitment.

Without the commitment to love in personal and public life, believers are not being faithful to our Lord.

## COMMITTING OURSELVES

*The study group members shift in their chairs and stretch a bit. John waits for their reactions.*

*Julia speaks first. "I do want to be committed to something bigger than myself. But too much commitment—isn't that kind of dangerous? I mean, like suicide bombers and cults and such."*

*Annette says, "My boyfriend and I have started going to church, but I don't want to become one of those people that stand on a street corner with a sign or give everything away and go off to some part of the world nobody's ever heard of. I hope he doesn't decide to do something like that." She goes blank for an instant, apparently imagining the worst.*

*"What about your commitment to each other?" Mike inquires.*

*"Oh, that's as strong as ever. Stronger. John, I really like what you said the Bible says about marriage. Most of it, anyway."*

*Julia seems impatient. "This thing Jesus taught about losing your life to save it—I can't buy that. I want to be myself. I don't want to dis-appear. I'd be afraid of losing myself completely in anything."*

John assures her, *"Christ doesn't mean for you to disappear. He made you. Why would he want you to disappear? It is a paradox, though. We do lose ourselves in a sense when we give ourselves to Christ and to other people. But we find ourselves too—our true selves. We find eternal life and joy in this present life. Jesus said he came to give abundant life, the fullest kind of life."*

Simon says thoughtfully, *"This idea of committing yourself to some-thing, I mean, to someone—"* he stumbles a little over the word— *"someone who is of infinite value—I have to admit, I do find it strangely attractive."*

Julia says, *"I know what you mean. So do I."*

*"I think my boyfriend might like this group,"* says Annette.

*"Bring him along,"* suggests Mike.

# LOVE AND CONSCIENCE

## Love Is Never Sane
## Apart from Conscience

*John glances at his watch for the third time. Mike has arrived and is making small talk, but where are the others? Tonight they're going to talk about an uncomfortable topic: sin and conscience.*

*John sees a flurry of motion. It's Julia, hurrying through the aisles with a shopping bag in hand. She arrives a bit breathless. "Had to get a birthday present for my nephew," she explains, pulling out a copy of a coffee-table book on classic sports cars. "He's crazy about these old cars. Just loves them."*

*They flip through the book as John keeps watching for the others in his peripheral vision. Simon strides in and seems about to explain his lateness when he spots the book on sports cars and sits down to peruse it also.*

*John is about to start without Annette when at last she arrives. "I tried to get Richard to come," she says. For a moment John doesn't understand her. Mike mutters in explanation, "The boyfriend." Now John takes full notice of how disturbed Annette looks, but he decides not to say anything about it. Simon reluctantly lets Julia stash away her nephew's book.*

*John begins, "Tonight we'll look at our third topic on love—*

*conscience. I hope to make a case for the idea that* love *is never sane* apart from conscience. *Also we'll look at a Bible passage where the apostle Paul wrote that he tried to always keep his conscience clear before God and before other people."*

*Julia immediately says, "Wait a minute. Wait a minute. You said love isn't sane apart from conscience. Are you saying love could be* insane?"

*Mike observes, "Well, you said your nephew was* crazy *about those old cars, didn't you? That he just* loves *them?"*

*"It's a figure of speech," says Julia.*

*"There's still truth in it," John says. "People justify a lot of crazy things in the name of love. Without clear guidelines, we can turn morality upside down. Right becomes wrong, and wrong becomes right, and love gets twisted."*

*"You Christians always want to force your morality on other people!" Simon protests. "That's why people feel guilty about so-called sins. They've violated somebody else's idea of right and wrong, and they feel guilty about it."*

*Annette nods. "I know what you mean. We've run into that in the church we go to. We can't tell certain people in that church that we're living together because they'd get all judgmental about it."*

*"We feel guilty when we have a false understanding of ourselves," Julia declares. "We're all perfect, if we only knew it. The problem is just that we don't know it."*

*Mike puts on an astonished look. "But Julia, if you're perfect, why in the world do you hang around with imperfect people like us?"*

*"That's not what I meant, and you know it!"*

*John tries to get the group back on topic. "Whether we use the word* perfect *or not, both atheism and New Age spirituality deny there is any objective, transcendent standard of good and evil. Atheism says morality is only a matter of personal preference or community prefer-*

ence. New Age spirituality says there are no ultimate distinctions, even between right and wrong. Either way, there's no such thing as sin. Therefore there's no need to feel guilty and no need for forgiveness."

"But don't you ever feel guilty about something?" Annette asks. "You wouldn't have a conscience if you didn't feel guilty sometimes." She looks around the group. No one seems willing to contradict her.

John responds, "If you're talking about the feeling that we've fallen short of some standard, then it's hard to get away from guilt. It's part of our everyday lives. But the real question is what standard we're talking about. If the standard is God's standard, I call it true guilt. If the standard is only cultural, it can result in what I call false guilt."

Mike asks, "So what do we do with false guilt? Ignore it?"

"No, you don't just ignore it. You smash it!" John responds. "You question those false standards on which it's based. With true guilt, though, you have to face it and deal with it somehow—which is what we'll be talking about today."

"But how are we supposed to know the difference between true guilt and false guilt?" Simon queries.

John says, "Let me tell you about the writer Franz Kafka."

## Spiritual Starvation

Just as some in John's group question whether there is true guilt, many nonbelievers have struggled to explain the guilt they experience. Some regard Franz Kafka as the representative atheist of the twentieth century. He was acutely aware of the human predicament, in which all deeply human aspirations are doomed to frustration. He summarized all of his writing this way: "There is a goal but there is no way." He desired to know why he felt guilty and wanted to get rid of the feeling. Surprisingly, he said that he understood original sin better than anyone, although his atheism provided no basis for anything to be sinful.[1]

Kafka wrote a novel called *The Trial*. In it Joseph K. is arrested on his thirtieth birthday, but he is never told his crime or how he can be acquitted of it. The whole novel has Joseph searching for the answers to two questions: *Why am I guilty?* and *How can I be acquitted?*

Joseph K. tries every source to answer the first question—the police, lawyers, judges—but nobody can tell him what he was arrested for. Then he tries to address the second question—acquittal. He even tries the church, but he is disappointed in the answers he receives. As in all Kafka stories, there is frustration from beginning to end. By the end of the novel, Joseph has turned himself inside out imagining all the things the authorities might have caught him doing. He feels very guilty, not knowing why, not knowing how to get rid of his guilt. His goal was freedom from guilt, but there was no way to get there.

Kafka also wrote a short piece called "A Hunger Artist," which was one of his favorite stories. It tells of a man who makes his living by professional fasting. The man does one forty-day fast after another. He has a manager who publicizes his fasting. They set up a cage, sometimes in the town square, and the "hunger artist," dressed in black tights, enters to some fanfare. The number of days remaining in the fast is then noted prominently on the cage. Toward the end of the forty days, people are encouraged to watch him around the clock in order to make sure he's not sneaking any food on the side. Finally at the end of the fortieth day, the manager hires a brass band and some beautiful women to usher the man out of the cage. People applaud and give money.

As time passes in the story, the noble art of fasting is no longer appreciated, and the hunger artist loses his manager. In order to continue his chosen profession, he has to persuade a circus to take him as a sideshow. He is placed in a cage between the big tent and the cages of the lions, tigers and elephants. When the show is over, people barely cast a glance at him sitting quietly in his cage. The circus manager even loses count of the number of days of the fast because he doesn't have to feed the man as he does the animals.

Finally, well past forty days, the circus manager finds the hunger artist, now just skin and bones, lying in the bottom of the cage. With his dying breath, he tells the manager his secret: "It wasn't that I liked to fast. If I could find any food that I liked, I would have stuffed myself like any of you, but I couldn't find any food that I liked." He dies; end of story. The story is a parable, not about physical hunger but about Kafka's spiritual hunger. He knew he was spiritually starving to death, but he couldn't find any food that he liked.

Kafka was honest about the dilemma in which he found himself—having a hunger that only a spiritual reality (God) could fill, yet not finding anything that satisfied him. I get the impression that the churches he saw around him didn't impress him as having a real spiritual vitality or an attractive love. There was nothing to persuade him that these churches had the answer he desperately desired.

## HAUNTED BY GUILT

Many people live a wild lifestyle but in the end are haunted by guilt over what they have become. One such person was writer Oscar Wilde. His story *The Picture of Dorian Gray* makes this point vividly. In it an artist paints a portrait of handsome young Dorian Gray. Dorian wishes for his appearance to remain the same, unaffected by his wild lifestyle. He wishes the damage to happen to the picture, not to himself. Dorian gets his wish. Every evil act or choice he makes changes the portrait, which is hidden in the attic, but does not change his own face.

One day the artist comes to visit Dorian and is appalled when he sees the portrait. He pleads with Dorian to change his ways. Instead, Dorian stabs the artist to death. Then he sees blood dripping down the picture. He grabs the knife, rips into the picture—and falls down dead. The picture returns to its original beauty, and the real Dorian lies dead, scarred by the effects of his evil ways. Whether or not Wilde intended this story to be about his own life, others clearly thought it applied to him. Certainly it does apply to people who try to rebel against God's ways and avoid the consequences.

Alfred Hitchcock made a tantalizing film about the conflict between relativistic ideology and reality. The movie, titled *Rope,* begins with two young men strangling a friend with a rope. They commit the murder to show their superiority and lack of captivity or subservience to any moral constraints, a relativistic philosophy they received from a professor at their college. In order to further show how they are above morality and guilt, the two host a dinner party and invite the dead friend's parents and girlfriend, as well as the professor. The friend's body is in a trunk in the center of the room. They even place food on the trunk. During the course of the evening, one of the young murderers begins to struggle with guilt and the fear of being caught. After the party ends, the professor comes back to the house. He puts things together and not only guesses what the young men did but where the body is. When the young men tell him that they were just putting into practice what he had taught them, he is horrified. When he sees the clear consequence of his views being played out in reality, he admits that he was wrong. It had been a theory, but seeing it in reality was too much for him. A person can *say* there is nothing intrinsically wrong and *say* there is no guilt, but it's another thing to face the real evils in this world or to see someone do something horrific because of those very beliefs.

Dostoyevsky's *The Brothers Karamazov* tells a similar story. The atheist brother maintains that if there is no God, everything is permitted. Yet when one of his brothers puts this philosophy into practice and kills their father, he is appalled. He suddenly recognizes that there is evil. And if there is evil, then there is good. And if there is good, then there is a standard for good—God.

## NO SUCH THING AS EVIL?

New Age spirituality denies that there is any guilt, sin or evil. I met with a top leader in the New Age movement who wrote a commentary on the book of Revelation—channeled, she said, by Jesus. In it she wrote, "You are perfect, O Humanity." She says that our only problem is that we don't realize we are perfect. Another booklet I came across has this idea of perfection as its central theme. If we just believed that we were perfect, all our guilt, fears and problems would disappear. Helen Schucman also claimed both of the volumes and the study guide that make up *A Course in Miracles* were dictated by Jesus. She denied that there is any guilt and said that we don't need the atonement of Jesus because we already have the "at-one-ment." One New Age author questions the Western world's taboo of incest. He argues that if we realize there are no distinctions anywhere, that all is one, then we will not hesitate to touch that which is really ourselves.

Susan, the college professor who spent years in the New Age movement, says she believed there was no sin and she could be good without religion. She would never say "I did something wrong." It was "never my fault." There was no evil. But Susan had a friend who for eight years kept asking her whether there was evil, which finally provoked her to consider other options, including Christ. During those years, it was "necessary for there not to be a reality, especially not a moral reality." One consequence of her denial of evil was regular bouts of depression.

## A BLAMELESS CONSCIENCE

By contrast, the biblical view places front and center the reasons why we are guilty and how we can be acquitted of it. The apostle Paul wrote, "I do my best always to have a clear conscience toward God and all people" (Acts 24:16 NRSV). Paul was careful not to offend God or other people. But in order to *keep* a clear conscience, you have to *get* one in the first place. Paul understood how far short of God's standard we all fall (Romans 3:9-23). We need to have our conscience cleansed and then strive to maintain a clear conscience, and we do this by confessing our sin, receiving forgiveness and resolving to avoid sin.

## LIFTING THE CLOUD OF GUILT

If we experience true guilt based upon God's standards, we can either deny it or acknowledge it as real and do something about it. If we deny our guilt and turn a blind eye to it, it will drain us of emotional energy and cast a thick fog over every aspect of our lives. If we face our guilt, acknowledge it, confess it and receive forgiveness, we can again have joy, freedom and clarity in our lives. The cloud is lifted; the fog is blown away, and peace with God is restored.

How well we live our spiritual lives depends greatly upon whether we get and keep a clear conscience. Conscience can be our greatest friend or our greatest enemy. Through our conscience, we experience either forgiveness or deep pangs of guilt. Little else brings joy like a sense of complete forgiveness, while nothing can plunge us into the depths of despair like an acute, unshakable sense of true guilt.

## ACHIEVING A CLEAR CONSCIENCE

Because a clear conscience is so instrumental to our emotional, spiritual and moral well-being, it is important that we know how to get one and keep one. Many think a clear conscience comes from just doing the right thing. While church reformer Martin Luther was a monk, he would spend five hours every day confessing his sin and would put himself through every discipline urged by his order, all in an effort to find peace of mind. Luther wrote:

> It's true; I was a good monk and kept my order so strictly that I could say that if ever a monk could get to heaven through monastic discipline, I should have entered in. All my companions in the monastery who knew me would bear out in this. For if I had gone on much longer, I would have martyred myself to death, what with vigils, prayers, readings and other works.

Despite all his efforts, Luther could not find peace for his conscience. He suffered from a bruised conscience. After having done everything according to the precepts of his order, he remained a tormented man; his conscience would not give him any assurance of salvation. He doubted whether he had performed his works correctly, whether he had repented enough or whether he had omitted something from his confession.

Not until Luther discovered "justification by faith in Christ alone" did he find peace for his troubled conscience. Unless gratitude for God's grace is a primary motive for our spiritual lives, some other motive, such as guilt, fear or mere duty, will dominate us.

The extent to which we develop into mature believers is determined by whether we are able to get and keep a clear conscience. If our conscience is at peace, everything looks different. English Puritan William Fenner argued:

> A good and quiet conscience makes a man taste sweetness in all outward things; in meat, in drink, in sleep, in the company of a good friend. . . . When the conscience is at peace, the soul is in good health, and so all things are enjoyed with sweetness and comfort. . . . The conscience is God's echo of peace to the soul in life, in death, in judgment it is an unspeakable comfort.[2]

Just as a good conscience touches every area of life with its benefits, so a guilty conscience can damage lives. A guilty conscience can make us avoid Scripture, forsake prayer and be less responsive to other people. It can affect our sleep and even dull the taste of our food.

## CONFESS AND BE FORGIVEN

Therefore, in addition to forgiveness of sins, we also need to regularly cleanse our conscience from sin by confessing to God and appropriating his forgiveness. Fenner said:

> We must everyday eye the brazen serpent. . . . Let us not sleep one night without a new pardon. Better sleep in a houseful of adders and venomous beasts than to sleep in one sin. O then be sure with the day to clear the sins of the day. Then shall our consciences have true peace.[3]

Getting and keeping a clear conscience makes a great difference in how we experience and live our lives. Above all, it means we have the right foundation for our lives—Christ. Luther said:

> This foundation is Christ alone before all good works, for he freely gives the foundation, peace to the conscience and trust to the heart. . . . This Christ Himself . . . gives us righteousness, peace, security of conscience that we might build on this by always acting well.[4]

Without the foundation of Christ, everything else in our lives will be much more difficult.

## WHAT IS CONSCIENCE?

In the New Testament, the Greek verb *synoida* means "to share the knowledge of" or "to be conscious of yourself." The word *syneidēsis,* translated *conscience,* means "to have a capacity to relate to yourself," especially looking back on your past. Conscience involves two things: (1) It judges whether something in our past has been done wrongly or rightly, causing a corresponding feeling of guilt or innocence. (2) It decides whether we will do something in the future. Conscience involves more than a theoretical consideration; it involves the application of knowledge to the deepest part of us.

There is no special word for *conscience* in the Old Testament, where the function of the conscience is attributed to the heart. After David, the king of ancient Israel, committed adultery with Bathsheba, he cried out, "Create in me a pure heart, O God, and renew a steadfast spirit within me" (Psalm 51:10). In these and other passages, the word *heart* is an all-purpose word that includes the functions of the conscience. In the New Testament, when the author of the letter to the Hebrews reflects on the faith and practices of his forefathers, he apparently uses Greek words for *heart* and *conscience* interchangeably (10:22).

## THE IMPORTANCE OF CONSCIENCE

The word *conscience* is used only 31 times in the New Testament, while the word *heart* (sometimes meaning *conscience*) is used 858 times in the Old Testament. But each time it is used in the New Testament, the word *conscience* appears with stunning significance.

In his letter to his young disciple Timothy, the apostle Paul gives the top three priorities of discipleship, mentoring or Christian education. He wrote, "The goal of this command is love, which comes from a pure heart and a good conscience and a sincere faith" (1 Timothy 1:5). Would we list a good conscience as one of the top goals of discipleship? Consider another statement by Paul: "I do my best always to have a clear conscience toward God and all people" (Acts 24:16 NRSV). How many of us make having a clear conscience a continual emphasis in our spiritual lives? While in custody in Jerusalem, Paul began his defense before the Jewish council by declaring, "Up to this day I have lived my life with a clear conscience before God" (Acts 23:1 NRSV). He wrote to Timothy to "fight the good fight, holding on to faith and a good conscience" (1 Timothy 1:18-19).

In the book of Hebrews, we read that the blood of Christ will "purify our conscience from dead works to worship the living God!" (Hebrews 9:14 NRSV). We are also invited to draw near to God "with a true heart in full assurance of faith, with our hearts sprinkled clean from an evil conscience" (Hebrews 10:22 NRSV). Because of Christ's high-priestly sacrifice on our behalf, "we are sure that we have a clear conscience" (Hebrews 13:18). Notice that in the first two passages, a cleansed conscience is a necessary pre-condition to serving and worshiping God.

## OVERCOMING OBSTACLES

As important as it is to gain "full assurance of faith," there are many practical obstacles to getting a clear conscience.

First, we need to develop an understanding of the doctrines of grace and forgiveness. Yet once we understand—and can even teach and write about these truths—we still need the help of God's Spirit to seal them on our conscience.

John Wesley was about forty years old before his heart was "strangely warmed" and he knew experientially that his sins were forgiven. C. S. Lewis was about fifty—twenty years after his conversion—before he knew the reality in his conscience of what his mind already grasped about the forgiveness of sins. Both Wesley and Lewis were knowledgeable and educated people of God, very influential in their times; yet they did not arrive at a complete experience of grace and forgiveness until they were older. A clear conscience is not dependent on works or knowledge. Once we understand what Christ has done for us, we need to pray for it to be applied to our conscience.

Second, we need to examine to what extent we believe or doubt. We may pray repeatedly for the forgiveness of a particular sin, not believing that God heard and answered us the first time. Should we stop praying? No. Instead, we should start praying for forgiveness for our unbelief. Do we believe that our sin is so big that even Christ's death on the cross cannot atone for it?

Third, we need to examine to what extent we are limited by our pride. Many of us are perfectionists in different areas of our lives. All perfectionists implicitly believe something along these lines: "I am unlimited, infinite and perfect, and I can ultimately be in control of my life." The antidote to perfectionism is to believe in the biblical view of creation, the Fall and redemption. In creation we are limited and finite; with respect to the Fall, we can say we are all imperfect; and certainly in redemption we see we cannot ultimately be in control of our lives because we need salvation from outside ourselves. Yet it is difficult for many people to say with conviction, "I am limited, finite and fallen, and I cannot ultimately be in control of my life."

I have heard it said that Christianity is both the easiest and the hardest religion. It is the easiest because all we need to do is say, "God, be merciful to me, a sinner." It is the hardest because enduring such humbling of our pride requires Herculean effort on our part.

What happens when we realize that we are imperfect and unable to live up to God's standard? Do we fall into despair? We should not. Instead, we should admit that we are totally dependent on Christ for salvation. Saving grace is by Christ alone, by grace alone and by faith alone. More than that, because we cannot earn God's grace, God gives it to us when we are ungodly. "You see, at just the right time, when we were still powerless, Christ died for the ungodly. . . . While we were still sinners, Christ died for us" (Romans 5:6, 8).

God took our sin and put it on Christ. He took Christ's perfection and put it on us. "God made him who had no sin to be sin for us, so that in him we might become the righteousness of God" (2 Corinthians 5:21). God's condemnation no longer hangs over our heads because "there is now no condemnation for those who are in Christ Jesus" (Romans 8:1). We will still feel the sting of sin's consequences and God's discipline as we seek to live this new life, but we will never be condemned or cast away from

God's presence. Our evil conscience is cleansed, and we receive a good, clear conscience.

## CONSCIENCE IS NOT AN INFALLIBLE GUIDE

Part of keeping a clear conscience is accurately understanding what is right or wrong. However, conscience is not an infallible guide. Conscience needs to be educated. Our duty may be clear, but because of sin our conscience can become defiled, seared or weak.

In fact, *we can come to believe that wrong is right.* In our culture we can see the effect of desensitizing the conscience so that what is wrong by God's standards is maintained to be right. The apostle Paul wrote of those whose "minds and consciences are corrupted" so that "they claim to know God, but by their actions they deny him" (Titus 1:15-16). We are bombarded on all sides by radio and television programs, movies, newspapers and magazines that present wrong as right. Our senses can be dulled to that which is right. You need to continually "be transformed by the renewing of your mind" so that you will not "conform any longer to the pattern of this world" (Romans 12:2).

*We can also come to believe that right is wrong.* Our conscience can also be dulled by becoming oversensitive. In this case, we may come to consider that what God calls right is actually wrong. The apostle Paul wrote:

> The Spirit clearly says that in later times some will abandon the faith and follow deceiving spirits and things taught by demons. Such teachings come through hypocritical liars, whose consciences have been seared as with a hot iron. They forbid people to marry and order them to abstain from certain foods, which God created to be received with thanksgiving by those

who believe and who know the truth. For everything God created is good, and nothing is to be rejected if it is received with thanksgiving, because it is consecrated by the word of God and prayer. (1 Timothy 4:1-5)

Notice Paul's strong language of warning: *abandon the faith, deceiving spirits, things taught by demons, hypocritical liars, consciences seared as with a hot iron.* But what is this horrible heresy that leads to such deplorable results? What is this terrible teaching? Essentially it is taking that which is good and acceptable and calling it bad and unacceptable. It is calling right wrong.

The advocates of the false teaching Paul was speaking of most likely forbade marriage because of a belief that our bodies and our sexuality are evil. They also advocated abstaining from food and were perhaps related to those who warned, "Do not handle! Do not taste! Do not touch!" (Colossians 2:21). They focused on what believers could *not* do. The problem was that they said no where God said yes. They made up rules where God had given no rules. They made up laws where God had left people free.

Paul's language about the *oversensitive* conscience is at least as strong, perhaps even stronger, than his words on *desensitizing* the conscience. Believers should guard and teach against the one extreme as much as the other.

*Moral education needs to be comprehensive and fearless.* All areas of personal and public life have intellectual and moral aspects. Augustine and many thinkers since have argued that *all truth is God's truth.* We are to learn everything we can about anything we can, realizing that it will lead back to the God of truth. B. B. Warfield argued:

We must not then as Christians assume an attitude of antagonism toward the truths of reason, or to the truths of philosophy, or the truths of science, or the truths of history, or the truths of criticism. As children of the light we must be careful to keep ourselves open to every ray of light. . . . Let us then cultivate an attitude of courage as over against the investigations of the day. . . . None should be more zealous in them than we. None should be quicker to discern truth in every field, more hospitable to receive it, more loyal to follow it, whithersoever it leads. It is not for Christians to be lukewarm in regard to the investigations and discoveries of the time. Rather as followers of the truth, indeed we can have no safety in science or in philosophy save in the arms of truth. It is for us, therefore, as Christians to push investigation to the utmost; to be leaders in every science; to stand in the van[guard] of criticism; to be the first to catch in every field the voice of the Revealer of truth who is also our Redeemer. The curse of the church has been her apathy to truth in which she has often left to her enemies that study of nature and of history and of philosophy and even that investigation of her own peculiar treasures, the Scriptures of God which should have been her chief concern. . . . She has nothing to fear from the truth; but she has everything to fear, and she already suffered nearly everything, from ignorance. All truth belongs to us as followers of Christ, the Truth; let us at length enter into our inheritance.[5]

We must educate our own conscience and that of our children with the truth God provides in the Word and in the world. Moral education must be presented in a loving manner. We are to speak the truth in love (Ephesians 4:15). Sometimes it is thought that truth divides and love unites. I would say rather that *truth is the root of love, and together they bring real and lasting unity.*

## TRUTH BETWEEN THE LINES

While speaking in high schools and colleges, I have met many students who were brought up in Christian homes where they were taught solid doctrine and morality but where family life was cold and lacking in love. There was an ugliness that made passionate commitment to Christ difficult, if not impossible. It was very hard for these students to separate the good things they learned from the bad taste left in their mouths. Not only in the home but also in our schools and churches, truth and goodness must be communicated in love in order to be compelling.

G. K. Chesterton argued that "education is implication." We primarily pick up not what is said explicitly but what is there between the lines. Learning is both taught and caught. Following the true and good is the most attractive way to live, and true moral education can take place only when the teacher models what is taught.

If we get a clear conscience, we have dealt with the guilt from our past. If we keep a clear conscience by confessing our sin regularly and attempting to avoid violating our conscience with respect to God or others, then we can be emotionally free to live in the present rather than in the past. The more we live in the present, the more available we are to love.

In fact, the more we experience unacknowledged and unconfessed guilt, the less we are able to love. Guilt over what we have done drains our energy and causes us to dwell in the past. The more we live in the past, the less energy we have to live in the present. In order to love, we need to be present. Unfortunately, we can be more absent than present. It is only by faith in what Christ has done on the cross that we can fully love. In Christ there is both an answer for why we are guilty and a solution for taking care of the guilt. Not only is our guilt addressed, but a foundation is laid for peace in our souls.

## SUMMARY

We all experience guilt.

Both atheism and New Age philosophy deny that there is real and objective guilt or sin, but then there is no way to know why we are guilty or how to get forgiveness.

At the very center of faith in Christ is getting and keeping a blameless conscience.

Getting a good conscience means knowing forgiveness.

Keeping a clear conscience means regularly confessing our sin and cleansing our conscience.

Keeping a clear conscience also involves educating our conscience so we can seek good and avoid evil.

This task of educating the conscience must be done in love.

Without conscience, right becomes wrong and wrong, right. Love—and life—then become insane.

## A COSMIC POINTER

*John looks around at the group members' faces. He had feared the subject would make them angry, but they all seem thoughtful.*

*With uncharacteristic hesitancy, Julia says, "I have to admit, sometimes I do feel guilty, but I don't know why. It's just kind of a vague feeling."*

*John asks her, "Do you think it could be because there's something written on your heart or conscience that tells you you're not on the right track? Blaise Pascal described it as a 'God-shaped vacuum' that only God can fill. John Calvin talked about a 'sense of deity' rooted in* us. C. S. Lewis talked about a desire for joy that causes us to long for more. Maybe our guilt is—well, let's call it a cosmic pointer to the nature of reality."

As Simon begins to respond, John expects him to say something sarcastic about the phrase "cosmic pointer to the nature of reality." Instead he refers to something John said earlier. "Those stories about Kafka and Wilde—I can't get those out of my head. Those guys both experienced guilt. But because they didn't believe in God, they couldn't fasten their guilt to something definite, so they couldn't shake it." He shakes his head. "But look, there are lots of other explanations for a guilty conscience besides breaking God's laws. We can feel guilty because of our upbringing or the expectations of society or even some kind of anxiety disorder."

John admits, "You're right. Most false guilt comes from how we were raised or some other aspects of our surroundings. The real question is whether there's really such a thing as true guilt. Is there actual evil for which we are accountable?"

"And you believe there is," says Simon. "Obviously."

"Put it this way. If there is no such thing as guilt or evil, then Christianity—and for that matter, Judaism and Islam—are all false. If, on the other hand, there is real evil and true guilt, then atheism, postmodernism, New Age spirituality and Neo-Paganism are all false because they have no way to account for such a thing."

"This is all so heavy and serious," Annette complains. "I thought talking about love would be more upbeat and positive. I'm not even sure what all this talk about guilt has to do with love anyway."

"Well," quips Mike, "we know you aren't married yet."

Most of the group laughs. Not Annette. She just stares at John.

John says, "I want to be positive, of course. But I also believe that what we think about conscience is very, very important. Partly because *it affects our ability to love. But also because what we do right now, in this life, counts forever."*

There is silence for a moment. Simon breaks it by asking, "What do you mean, forever? You mean if we blow it, there's no hope? Don't you believe your God forgives you?"

"Absolutely. God does forgives us, if we accept his mercy in Christ. But if we don't deal with our guilt—and I'm talking about true guilt, not just our guilty feelings—then it counts forever. On the other hand, God remembers our good acts forever too—especially our acts of love. The Bible says in 1 Corinthians 15:58 that nothing we do for the Lord is in vain." He lays down his pen. "And that, folks, is the end of our time."

Thoughtfully, one by one, the group members get up and leave. Julia almost forgets her nephew's book. Mike looks regretfully at his half cup of cold coffee. Simon carefully slides his chair back under the table as though trying to make things square and precise. Annette seems about to ask John something, but then turns away and leaves the bookstore.

# LOVE AND CHARACTER

## Love Is Never Safe
## Apart from Character

*"I'm eager to get our discussion going this evening,"* John *says when everyone has arrived. "I think we'll have some controversy but also some agreement."*

*"Sounds normal for us,"* Mike *observes.*

John *continues, "Tonight we're going to address the topic of character and how character affects the ability to love. We'll consider the idea that love is never safe apart from character. We'll also look at Jesus' teaching on contrasting ways of life in Matthew 7 and ask what's unique about Christ-centered character."*

Julia, *who has been taking a sip of tea, sets down her mug. "There you go again, John. Are you saying people can't have character unless they believe in Jesus Christ?"*

*"No, I'm not. Anyone can have character. All you need to do is choose some values and hold firmly to them. But I am saying there's something unique about Christ-centered character. Something—"*

*"But I just don't think that's true. I mean, every religion—"*

*"Let the man finish his thought." Simon turns to John. "All right. Tell us why Christian character is so special."*

John *smiles. "I would say that Christ-centered character involves a* heart that's been changed by God. Instead of being controlled by our own selfishness, we start to be directed by love for God and others, especially by what the Bible calls agape love."

Annette, who has been rather quiet, perks up. "Did you say agape? I've heard that word in church. What's it mean exactly?"

"Well, agape is one of several words for love in the Greek language."

Simon asks, "So? Anybody here speak Greek?"

John expects Mike to say "It's all Greek to me," but he doesn't, so John continues. "It's the language in which the New Testament was written. The Greek word agape wasn't even commonly used before the New Testament. It means the kind of love that is completely other-centered—essentially, the sacrifice of self in the service of someone else."

Simon shakes his head. "Well, that's a nice romantic notion, but it's not the way life really works. I mean, look at the natural world. It's all survival of the fittest—eat or be eaten."

John answers quickly, "You're right. Charles Darwin even said that any truly other-directed trait would negate the theory of evolution. Natural selection couldn't produce it. Richard Dawkins goes even further and says that universal love does not make evolutionary sense."

Annette points out, "But animals show love for their own young. They'll even sacrifice themselves to save their babies. So there must be some biological explanation for love."

John says, "Some biologists try to explain love in terms of family loyalty, that you make sacrifices in order to preserve your own kin. Or there's an innate biological drive to preserve the species. Or there's the idea of mutual benefit—if I scratch your back, you might scratch mine."

"Except that's not really love, is it?" asks Annette.

*John nods. "I certainly think all those answers have problems of their own. The most disturbing part is that a strictly naturalistic, evolutionary viewpoint has no place for other-centered agape love, which means it has no place for human rights. Let's take a further look."*

## NO ROOM FOR ALTRUISM

Because naturalism denies objective moral values, there is no place for altruism or other-centered love. One materialist scholar says, "No hint of genuine charity ameliorates our vision of society."[1] Another scholar sums up the essence of evolutionary biology: "What's in it for me is an ancient refrain for all life."[2] Richard Dawkins says, "Universal love and the welfare of the species as a whole are concepts which simply do not make evolutionary sense."[3]

Darwin maintained that any truly other-centered trait "would annihilate my theory, for such could not have been produced by natural selection."[4] He maintained that the natural world does not contain—in fact, could not contain—any genuinely self-disinterested goodness. Therefore, some explain any love we have for family that transcends our individual selfishness as a drive for the survival of our own genes. Others say we pretend to be loving so we can get something from others—a kind of reciprocal love based in self-interest. Certainly much tit-for-tat "loving" does go on, but it is not genuine, sacrificial love.

Recently I met with a professor who speaks and writes widely on evolutionary biology. He has a unique argument that he has developed over his years of study. You might call it the argument from agape. Basically he points out that there is currently no strictly Darwinian understanding of how to get to altruistic, truly other-centered, agape love. There is, he says, a growing recognition that materialist genetic explanations are not fully adequate to account for altruistic love. For instance, Richard Dawkins admits on the last page of *The Selfish Gene* that we alone in the universe are capable of altruism. It is something that has no place in nature. Dawkins speaks of "disinterested altruism—something that has no place in nature, something that has never existed before in the whole history of the world."[5] Because of this admission, he has to give up or supplement his genetic materialism.

Materialism entails a couple of central ideas: (1) All things are determined or facilitated by physical, material causes. (2) All genes established by natural selection produce behaviors that benefit the individual. To use a double negative, no gene produces behaviors that fail to benefit the survival of that gene. This means that any truly self-sacrificial trait is excluded. But it still seems that there is selfless, altruistic, other-centered love. How can a Darwinian explanation account for this phenomenon?

There have been various attempts to accommodate this quandary. First, the idea of kinship encourages suffering or death to protect members of the immediate family, who share genes. But this explanation is of limited scope and value in the debate because it does not apply to those outside the family (immediate or extended). Second, there is a direct reciprocal argument. You could sacrifice for those from whom you would expect to get an equal or better sacrifice—you could even call it a fair trade. Third, there is an indirect reciprocal argument that such "selfless" acts are done so that you appear good in the community's eyes, thus benefiting eventually.

But can all human acts be reduced to ultimately self-benefiting actions? These theories only rise as high as the principle that you "love those who love you" (Matthew 5:46). Jesus calls believers to go beyond this kind of love, to love our enemies or those we don't know and may never see again. This kind of love goes beyond anything materialism can explain.

In fact, Dawkins knows that humans are capable of altruistic love, as we saw earlier. How does he explain his materialism and the "selfish gene"? The professor I spoke with maintains that Dawkins gives up pure genetic materialism. Dawkins postulates that, in addition to genes, there exist *memes*—nonmaterial entities that infect the human mind and make people do what they wouldn't do otherwise. These memes seem to hop from person to person like a virus. Dawkins makes up this vague, unsubstantiated, unverified meme to explain things like religion or agape love. The professor raises the somewhat facetious question, "How is a meme—something that inhabits human minds and makes people behave in ways their biology can't explain—different from a demon? Or the Holy Spirit?" In fact, Dawkins calls altruistic actions that are not done to kin or that are not motivated by direct or indirect reciprocal benefits *misfires* or *Darwinian mistakes*.[6] It is equivalent, Dawkins says, to this kind of scenario: when a mother bird returns to her nest with food, her instinct tells her to put the food in whatever gaping mouths she sees, without noticing that another species of bird has mistakenly gotten into the nest. Thus, all of the most noble, self-sacrificing deeds of humanity are reduced to dropping worms into the wrong genetic mouths. Agape love is a genetic misfiring or a Darwinian mistake. Is not such an account suspect?

Many atheists are nihilists (believing there is no purpose for life, there are no morals, etc.), but they don't like the implications of such a position. For instance, David Sloan Wilson's book *Darwin's Cathedral* values religion's effective promotion of commitment and community. Wilson says beliefs of religious people are wise—but false. They are practical "truths" that have beneficial results for society, but they have no basis in reality. Michael Ruse argues in his book *Taking Darwin Seriously* that moral realism has to be jettisoned. When asked whether he could give any place for morality, Ruse replied that he acted on the basis of sheer preference: "What's right is what I feel is right."

The professor I spoke with concluded that it is of some value to critique the implications of evolutionary nihilism and related attempts to reduce things like morality and love to self-interest. However, the best way to disprove this view of life is to act in an agape way—to love our enemies, to give sacrificially without any thought of return, to love as Jesus loved. Thus we can demonstrate in these loving actions something that materialistic theories can't explain. People recognize that when they encounter such love, they are encountering something unusual. You can show Darwinian materialism to be false by your love.

The naturalistic, materialistic view of the world offers no basis for intrinsic human dignity. There is no adequate reason to say that human beings are worth more than animals, plants or rocks, or have a unique responsibility for them. Despite attempts to construct a moral system without God, such as the social contract theory or utilitarianism, atheism offers no basis for objective moral values other than preference, whether personal or communal.

## WHERE DOES CHARACTER COME FROM?

If there is no basis for moral values, human dignity or love, where is there a basis for character? Many atheists borrow values drawn from the biblical system, such as justice, dignity and caring, and try to justify these values without God. Nietzsche said it all comes down to a "will to power"; break conventional values and construct your own. On what basis can an atheist say that Nietzsche's quest for a "superman" (who would create his own values) or a "super-race" (that would not follow a herd morality) is wrong? Why should we not just invent our own morality?

Like atheism, New Age spirituality is morally relativistic. New Age philosophy strongly repudiates any concept of right or wrong, good or evil. Zen Buddhist master Yun Men maintained, "I want you to get the plain truth; be not concerned with right and wrong; the conflict between right and wrong is sickness of the mind."[7]

Hermann Hesse in *Siddhartha* puts forth a similar view: "The world, Govinda, is not imperfect or slowly evolving along a path to perfection. No, it is perfect at any moment. . . . Therefore, it seems to me that everything that exists is good—death as well as life, sin as well as holiness, wisdom as well as folly!"[8]

Journalist Arthur Koestler once interviewed a Japanese expert on Buddhism:

> Koestler: "You favor tolerance towards all religious and political systems. What about Hitler's gas chambers?"
>
> Buddhist: "That was very silly of him."
>
> Koestler: "Just silly, not evil?"
>
> Buddhist: "Evil is a Christian concept. Good and evil exist only on a relative scale."[9]

## WHAT ABOUT KARMA?

Do reincarnation and the related idea of good and bad karma provide a basis for ethics? I think not, because the all-is-One principle of nondistinction provides no basis for any meaningful distinction between good karma and bad karma. The more philosophically consistent an Eastern advocate is, the less emphasis is placed on karma. If we say there is no distinction between good and evil, then we cannot say that the distinction between good and bad karma matters in the next life.

Susan, the ex-New Age college professor, recalls that she denied the concepts of sin and evil. She thought human beings were in our present predicament because we got rid of the sacred feminine. Although she talked of love, it was very abstract. It was important to "pretend that things are the way that they are not." By this method she could put herself in the position where her image of herself (as perfect) could be reinforced. She said that she was "always in another world in her mind."

Again let me stress that I have talked to many followers of New Age spirituality, and I have found that they are trustworthy people with many outstanding character traits. Both in conversation and in writing, they condemn injustice and evil in public life. What I do question is whether their worldview offers any philosophical basis for character, moral values or other-centered love—or any hope for a final resolution of such issues.

## UNIQUELY CHRISTIAN LOVE

By contrast, the biblical view of character is grounded in love. Amos N. Wilder wrote that "agape is in effect a Christian creation."[10] The word *agape* is only used one other time in early Greek literature, yet this kind of love is placed front and center in the New Testament. In the Judaism of Jesus' time, God was so holy and remote that one would never think of approaching such a God in a familiar manner. The name of God was forbidden to even be pronounced and was written without the vowels (YHWH). The Jewish

Targums sometimes used the phrase "word of God" instead of even writing the holy consonants.

In the Greek culture, the gods were not exactly generous. You might even call them grudging. For instance, Prometheus was said to steal fire from heaven to give to men. Consequently, Zeus was angry, so he chained Prometheus to a rock and sent a vulture to tear out his liver every day (sadly for Prometheus, it grew back). As this example shows, the Greeks experienced continual hostility between the gods and men.

These gods were also incapable of being known to man. Plato said that it was difficult to find out about God and impossible to tell anyone else about him (even if you did discover something). To Plutarch, all we could expect was a flash of illumination. He said, "To whom then shall I recite my prayers? To whom tender vows? To whom slay victims? To whom shall I call to help the wretched, to favor the good, to counter the evil?" The gods were beyond men.

In Epicurean philosophy, the gods were beings without care. The gods enjoyed *ataraxia*—perfect serenity undisturbed by earthly events and utterly detached from them. The Stoics believed in a god of *apatheia*—totally incapable of feeling—a god without heart.

Into this cultural context came the message of God's self-revelation in his Son, Jesus Christ. God not only revealed himself through Christ's life here on earth, but he showed, definitively, that he wants to be in a relationship with us. Jesus invited disciples to follow him, and he desired to forgive and love them. Jesus didn't avoid sinners but sought them out. Jewish liberal scholar C. G. Montefiore says, "So far as we can tell, this pity for the sinner was a new note in religious history."[11] This idea of a God who seeks (as in the lost sheep, the lost coin and the two lost sons) is unparalleled in any other religious perspective. God not only loves humankind, but he loves each one of us individually. Augustine says, "God loves each one of us as if there was only one of us to love."[12] This is a staggering revelation, easy to say, but sometimes difficult to appropriate into our experience.

The idea of agape love that extends even to the unlovable was chosen by Christians as a key contrast to the kind of love reserved only for the lovely. Agape is unmotivated by any moral beauty in the one who is loved, while *eros* (romantic love) and *philia* (friendship) are motivated by beauty or virtue in the loved one. Agape love gives without any desire for something in return.

The truly unique contribution of Christianity, one not found in nonbiblical religions, is the idea that *God is love*. Leon Morris says in his study of love:

> Why does God love sinners? I have been arguing that He loves them because it is in His nature to love, because He is love. Unceasingly, He gives in spontaneous love. He loves not because of what we are but because of what He is: He is love. This is a new and distinct idea in Christianity, though in part of the Old Testament (notably in Hosea), we read about something very much like it. But it is not found in the nonbiblical traditions.[13]

Emil Brunner uses the analogy of radium. You could mention all kinds of properties of radium—its molecular structure, chemical properties and so on; but if you failed to say that it *radiates,* you would miss something essential.[14] Similarly, you could list God's many attributes—holiness, justice, goodness, omniscience and omnipotence; but if you were to omit that he constantly gives himself in love—in fact, that he *is* love—you would miss that which really matters.

The primary reason followers of Christ love is that God first loved us. Brunner writes:

> The message that God is love is wholly new in the world. We perceive this if we try to apply the statement to the divinities of the various religions of the world: Wotan is love; Zeus, Brahma, Ahura Mazda, Vishnu, Allah is love. All these combinations are obviously wholly impossible. Even the God of Plato, who is the principle of all Good, is not Love. Plato would have met the statement "God is Love" with a bewildered shake of the head. From the standpoint of his thought, such a statement would have been utter nonsense.[15]

## CULTURAL CHARACTER INITIATIVES

In the modern cultural attempt to teach character without God, love is almost always lacking. A number of groups, however, have attempted such a task. For example, the Character Counts Coalition lists these pillars of character: respect, responsibility, trustworthiness, justice, fairness, caring, civic virtue and citizenship.[16] The Community of Caring affirms "five core values—caring, respect, trust, responsibility, and family."[17] The Character Education Institute focuses on "universal values" such as courage, honesty, truthfulness, justice, tolerance, honor, generosity, kindness, helpfulness, freedom of choice, equal opportunity and economic security. The Heartwood Institute, based in Pittsburgh, stands out as an exception by including love as one of the "seven universal attributes along with courage, loyalty, justice, respect, hope, and honesty."[18]

The problem with character education without God is that once you strip good character of its theological foundation, there

is no solid reason *why* you ought to be the kind of person pre-
scribed. James Davison Hunter, in his insightful book *The Death
of Character,* points out that the "demise of character begins with
the destruction of creeds, the convictions, and the 'god terms'
that made those creeds sacred to us and inviolable within us."[19]
Once values are stripped of their "commanding character," then
the word *value* is reduced to utility, personal preference or community consensus. Hunter argues that contemporary moral education, as well intended as it may be, actually "undermines the
capacity to form the convictions upon which character must be
based if it is to exist at all."[20] We are desperately seeking a re-
newal of character but are not willing to give it a sufficient foundation. Hunter writes:

> We say we want a renewal of character in our day but don't
> really know what we ask for. To have a renewal of character
> is to have a renewal of a creedal order that constrains, limits,
> binds, obligates, and compels. This price is too high for us
> to pay. We want character but without unyielding convic-
> tion; we want strong morality but without the emotional
> burden of guilt or shame; we want virtue but without par-
> ticular moral justifications that invariably offend; we want
> good without having to name evil; we want decency without
> the authority to insist upon it; we want more community
> without any limitations to personal freedom. In short we
> want what we cannot possibly have on the terms that we
> want it.[21]

Omitting love not only deprives character of coherence; it deprives character of motive, rooted in the love of God as demonstrated in Christ and commanded by him.

## THE RISK OF LOVE

How can we risk loving friends, spouses, coworkers, neighbors and fellow citizens? Sometimes we are called to love without regard for our own safety, as when we obey Christ's command to love our enemies (Matthew 5:44). Yet it is wise before entering into a long-term relationship to consider the other person's character. We need to exercise godly caution and wisdom when entering into friendships, marriage and business partnerships. Love in a relationship is safe only when character is present.

For example, a habitually abusive spouse may do an occasional good deed, but it is not safe to be in a relationship with him or her. A church is not safe apart from the character of its members. A business partnership is only as safe as the character of the partners. A nation is only as safe as the character of its citizens. You can trust wisely only when you discern that good character is present.

*Relationships can rise only as high as the character of those involved.* Plato argued that you cannot be good friends with a bad person because sooner or later your friend's bad character will manifest itself. Your relationship will rise only as high as the lowest level of character between the two of you.

## THREE KINDS OF FRIENDSHIP

Aristotle argued that there are three kinds of friendship: utility, pleasure and virtue. Only the friendship of virtue can be trusted to rise to the heights because it is the only one based on unchanging values.

Friendships of utility are based upon a common situation, such as working at a summer camp, playing on a sports team or working at the same job. They can be of great value, but it is unrealistic to expect that all of these relationships will continue beyond the common context in which they grow. If the relationship is primarily about playing basketball together, it is likely that if you meet again later in life, the only thing you will have in common is basketball. If you work together at a summer camp, the friendship is based on accomplishing the task of running the camp. Outside that context, there is little else to bind the relationship.

The second category of Aristotle's friendships is friendship of pleasure, which is based upon common good times you have had together. Fun times in high school and college often draw people together and create good memories. However, if the friendship is not based on something more than pleasure, then if you meet again years later, you may be able to talk only about the good old times. Such conversations are common at high school and college reunions.

Of course, it is good to have friendships of utility and pleasure, as long as you do not expect more of those relationships than they can deliver. Proverbs 17:17 says, "A friend loves at all times, and a brother is born for adversity."

A true friend is *with* you and *for* you despite changing situations and circumstances. When good times change to times of adversity, a true friend continues to love. It seems that a true friend was *born* just to help in that time of adversity. But that is not true of all friendships.

Only the third type of friendship, the friendship of virtue, can survive changing contexts and calamities. Because the friendship of virtue is based on that which is eternal and unchanging—the true, the good and the beautiful—it lasts no matter what. If Aristotle pursued such a lasting friendship of virtue, how much more should Christians, whose friendships are based on the unchanging Christ? If you meet your friend years later, and you have both been pursuing the unchanging Christ, you can pick up right where you left off.

Recently I spent time with an old friend whom I had not seen much in the three decades since our days working together in Young Life, a Christian ministry to high school students. Because we both had continued to follow Christ, study his Word and pursue ministry, there was still a bond between us. Our conversation flowed easily and naturally to eternal things, permanent things—what we can call *first things*. Relationships based on first things will withstand the storms of life. Only relationships based on that which is unchanging have a solid basis to withstand life's constant changes.

## DISCERNING CHARACTER

*To discern a person's character, look at whomever that person has treated or is treating most poorly, and you will see the degree to which his or her character can descend.* It is not wise to trust that person beyond that level of their character. Given enough time and opportunity, what they do to another they will likely do to you. The book of Proverbs warns us to distinguish between people who pretend to be our friend and those who are the real thing: "Some friends play at friendship but a true friend sticks closer than one's nearest kin" (Proverbs 18:24 NRSV).

## FORGIVENESS VS. TRUST

Because of my background in dealing with religious cults, I was called to go to a city where a leader had abused a small group of followers. After years of exploiting his position in order to get money, sex and power, he was finally found out. His little flock was in dismay. How could their trusted leader have been so abusive in manipulating people, having many adulterous affairs and mishandling finances? He pleaded with them to forgive him and trust him

again. As I worked with the group, together we came to this conclusion: Forgiveness? Yes. Trust? No!

Christ calls us to forgive when anyone asks. We do not have
the option to hold on to bitterness and resentment. When someone asks to be forgiven, we must forgive (although we may
choose to discuss the amount of pain caused by the offense). But
Christ does not call us to trust everyone equally. For the
wounded members of the group I met with, it would be wise to
trust that leader again only after he had demonstrated over time
that he had changed his ways.

Often believers assume that a person who claims to be a Christian should be trusted more than another person. If only it were
true! But it is not. Believers are forgiven for their sin, but we all
come to Christ with various character deficiencies. Our faults do
not automatically disappear. By the Holy Spirit, our new birth in
Christ brings us renewed desires and scriptural guidelines for our
actions. But being born again does not mean that love and good
deeds immediately abound. Often we must do battle equipped
with the "full armor of God" (Ephesians 6:11) to overcome bitterness, lust, envy, pride and other vices. Wise leaders and followers
need to be discerning about those to whom they entrust responsibility. Do they demonstrate the level of character appropriate for
the responsibility to be given them?

## A PATTERN OF CHOICES

Character assumes that our individual actions are not done in isolation from each other. Character is the pattern of choices that
flow out of a person. The pattern can be one of vices or one of virtues. Character assumes consistency, integrity and dependability
in our actions. In his groundbreaking work *Character in the Chris-*

*tian Life,* Stanley Hauerwas wrote: "To stress the significance of the idea of character is to be normatively committed to the idea that it is better for men to shape rather than be shaped by their circumstances."[22]

It is fine to look at each individual action and judge whether it is right or wrong, sin or not sin. But by focusing on the sinfulness of individual behaviors, believers often neglect to consider how to deal with deeply entrenched vices. Each individual action reinforces a previous pattern, and each action shapes the self in an accustomed fashion or sets a new path. We do not at each moment invent ourselves anew. Perhaps that is why Jesus spoke not only of individual actions but of a way of life.

Over and over again in the Gospels, Jesus talks about the *either-or*. There are two ways, and only two. "Enter through the narrow gate. For wide is the gate and broad is the road that leads to destruction, and many enter through it. But small is the gate and narrow the road that leads to life, and only a few find it" (Matthew 7:13-14). There are two ways—the broad and the narrow—and we are all headed down one path or the other.

In the same way, there are only two kinds of character. Jesus uses two trees to illustrate this point: "Every good tree bears good fruit, but a bad tree bears bad fruit. A good tree cannot bear bad fruit, and a bad tree cannot bear good fruit. Every tree that does not bear good fruit is cut down and thrown into the fire. Thus, by their fruit you will recognize them" (Matthew 7:17-20).

Jesus also indicates that the kind of fruit is determined by the kind of tree. "Do people pick grapes from thornbushes, or figs from thistles?" (Matthew 7:16). You do not get blueberries from an apple tree or peaches from an orange tree. The character of the tree determines the kind of fruit produced. A fundamentally good tree could occasionally produce bad fruit, but a bad tree will consistently produce bad fruit.

## SAND AND ROCK

Only two foundations can be laid—one on the rock of Christ and one on the sand of anything else—as Jesus illustrates in this parable:

> Therefore everyone who hears these words of mine and puts them into practice is like a wise man who built his house on the rock. The rain came down, the streams rose, and the winds blew and beat against that house; yet it did not fall, because it had its foundation on the rock. But everyone who hears these words of mine and does not put them into practice is like a foolish man who built his house on sand. The rain came down, the streams rose, and the winds blew and beat against that house, and it fell with a great crash. (Matthew 7:24-27)

Repeated actions of obedience build a person's life on the foundation of rock. Repeated acts of disobedience mean a person's life will be blown away when the storms of life come.

C. S. Lewis wrote that every act we do makes a little mark on our soul, sending us down one path or the other toward what he called the *beatific* vision or the *miserific* vision, that is, toward happiness or misery. Lewis wrote:

> Every time you make a choice, you are turning the central part of you, the part that chooses, into something a little different from what it was before. . . . You are slowly turning this central thing either into a heavenly creature or a hellish crea-

ture. . . . To be one kind of creature is heaven: that is joy and peace and knowledge and power. To be the other means madness, horror, idiocy, rage, impotence and eternal loneliness. Each of us at each moment is progressing to one state or the other.[23]

## CULTIVATING CHARACTER

*While we may imagine that character is a matter of big heroic actions, character is won or lost in the little things.* A classic saying defines the process:

Sow a thought, reap an act.
Sow an act, reap a habit.
Sow a habit, reap a character.
Sow a character, reap a destiny.

Our thoughts influence our actions. Our actions form entrenched patterns of habit that tend toward virtue or vice. The sum total of our virtues and vices is our character. And our character certainly influences our destiny.

To borrow an old saying (my own variation):

For want of a thought, an act is lost.
For want of an act, a habit is lost.
For want of a habit, a character is lost.
For want of a character, a destiny is lost.

I was an instructor for Prison Fellowship for a number of years, traveling to numerous prisons throughout the country to give seminars. Often I would be inside a prison for twelve hours at a time. During breaks and meals, I had the opportunity to hear inmates' stories.

One inmate had been a pharmacist. He once sold a drug without a prescription to someone who asked him for it. Over time, that first sale led to numerous sales and a pattern of drug dealing. He told me that when he first sold a drug illegally, he never imagined he would end up in prison.

At another prison I met a pastor. His wife had become involved in an adulterous affair. When the pastor found out, he was so angry that he wanted revenge. So he went to see a prostitute. He saw her again and again. That led to more relationships in the underworld of prostitution and drugs. He began to get involved in pushing women and drugs, and rumors of his involvement spread. One day after he had preached his sermon at church, a nine-year-old girl walked up to him and said, "My mom says you are the best preacher in the whole world, but I don't see how you can be the best preacher and do the things that you do." Her comment devastated him. He was appalled to realize how far he had fallen. For about a week, he scarcely got out of bed. He repented of his sin, but he had to go to prison for the crimes he had committed. This pastor's destiny was profoundly altered by that first little thought of revenge and his consequent choice to act on it. He went down the road a long way before he turned back.

## SOW A THOUGHT, REAP AN ACT

Deciding what goes into our minds is the beginning of building *character.* The Bible has a lot to say about the importance of our thoughts. The apostle Paul urged believers, "Do not conform any longer to the pattern of this world, but be transformed by the renewing of your mind" (Romans 12:2). One of the first steps in our transformation involves rejecting thoughts from our cultural environment that are opposed to Christ. Rather than conforming to the world's pattern of thinking, we should pursue the renewing of our minds.

Prior to coming to Christ, we are enslaved to sin, "gratifying the cravings of our sinful nature and following its desires and thoughts" (Ephesians 2:3) Not only the flesh but the *mind* is in captivity. Jesus says, "Out of the abundance of the heart the mouth speaks. The good person brings good things out of a good treasure, and the evil person brings evil things out of an evil treasure. I tell you, on the day of judgment you will have to give an account for every careless word you utter" (Matthew 12:34-36 NRSV). Good thoughts and good words flow out of a good heart, while evil words flow out of evil in the heart. The treasure of good thoughts filling the heart spills over into good words and good actions.

In a familiar and much-loved verse, Paul advises, "Whatever is true, whatever is noble, whatever is right, whatever is pure, whatever is lovely, whatever is admirable—if anything is excellent or praiseworthy—think about such things" (Philippians 4:8). We need to guard our hearts and minds because out of these come our words and actions.

## SOW AN ACT, REAP A HABIT

When we act rightly and continue in that pattern, we form *virtues*. On the other hand, when we act wrongly and continue in that pattern, we develop vices. Bad habits can easily be stopped in their beginnings. However, the longer we practice bad habits, the stronger they become. In the beginning, bad habits are like cobwebs— sticky and unpleasant but easily broken. If we do not resist them, bad habits become chains that bind us. We usually use the word *addiction* in a negative sense, but William Glasser argued in his book *Positive Addiction* that some practices, though habit forming, can be good—perhaps just another way of explaining virtues.[24]

A psychiatrist friend, Dr. David Allen, was one of the first to work on treating crack cocaine addicts. He said that crack cocaine is the one drug that must never be tried because it is almost 100 percent addictive. On the first try, it delivers the highest high you could imagine. Addicts have described it as having a thousand orgasms or having Christmas every day. But because of the depletion of a certain chemical in the brain, the user will never get the same high again. The second high is always less than the first, the third less than the second and so on. Addicts have said that they could "see" the first high from the second, but they could not get there. After a while, the addict gets very little pleasure from the cocaine and is instead attacked by cocaine depression, then withdrawal if the drug is not continued.

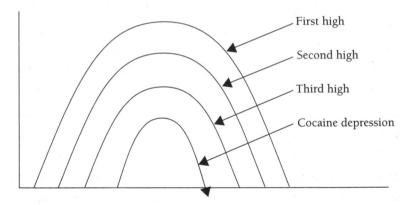

The phenomenon of diminishing returns is a picture of what happens with all sinful habits. Initially the act is filled with pleasure, but not too far down the road comes the tyranny of addiction and increasing loss of pleasure. The initial pleasure is a hook that draws the person in. It is better to stop the habit in the beginning—or, as with crack cocaine, to never begin it at all.

## SOW A HABIT, REAP A CHARACTER

Hebrews 5:14 describes the character-building process: "Solid food is for the mature, who by constant use have trained themselves to distinguish good from evil." First, we must take in solid food instead of milk, meaning in-depth teaching rather than only the basics (Hebrews 5:12-14). Second, our good thoughts should not stay in our mind but be put into practice regularly so they become habitual and we develop the characteristic of wisdom. Then we will be trained to discern good and evil. We need solid biblical content and the regular practice of it in order to produce Christlike character.

## SOW A CHARACTER, REAP A DESTINY

Character flaws can profoundly affect people's destiny. A wrong word or phrase can destroy the careers of radio and television announcers. Politicians who let go a slip of the tongue can lose power and position. I once heard this proverb: *A slip of the tongue leads to a slip of the mind, which leads to a slip of the soul.* Something wrong slips out of the tongue, and pride leads us to rationalize it and justify it—the slip of the mind. Our denial of our original mistake leads to the slip of the soul.

Destiny is like a diet—it is won or lost in the little things. I may start with great resolve, having orange juice and a piece of toast without butter for breakfast. Lunch consists of a small piece of broiled chicken and a salad without dressing. For an afternoon snack, I have one Oreo cookie. Later in the afternoon, I have the rest of the package. For dinner there is a large pizza with everything on it and a whole cheesecake for dessert. You get the idea. What is the problem with just one Oreo cookie? Nothing, really; I have even heard that you could lose weight on a diet of Oreo cookies if you did not eat too many. The problem is that our resolve is easily broken. It takes only a moment of irresolution to alter our destiny.

## CHARACTER EROSION

For ten years the C. S. Lewis Institute offered a summer program on the eastern shore of Chesapeake Bay. The property was expensive to maintain, and the least obvious things were the most expensive. Around the edge of the property was a seawall that cost tens of thousands of dollars to install. Yet it was necessary; the owner of the adjacent property had not spent the money to build a seawall and as a result lost several acres of valuable land to the bay.

Erosion is a perennial problem on shorelines as well as in our spiritual lives. When we neglect time in Scripture and time in prayer, we do not always see or feel immediate negative consequences. It may take time before the erosion is evident.

On Chesapeake Bay property, there is a house not far from the shore. Without the seawall, the house would fall into the bay. Maybe it wouldn't happen this year or next year, maybe not even in five or ten years; but sooner or later that house would be destroyed. People often fall in private before they fall in public. Prayer will drive out sin, or sin will drive out prayer. The erosion, unless battled, is relentless.

Another problem on this Chesapeake Bay property is accumulation of silt. There was a time that large boats could come right up the channel and dock in the harbor; but because of silt accumulation, the channel needs to be dredged, a difficult and expensive project. In the same way, our lives can accumulate "silt," which muddies the waters and makes it difficult for us to see clearly. Periodically we need to dredge the channel so clear water can flow again and we can restore clear communication with our Lord. Once the dredging is done, it must be maintained, or silt will accumulate again.

## LITTLE DECISIONS PREVIOUSLY MADE

We can prepare for heroic acts by living our ordinary lives well. The best preparation for the big moments of life is all of the little moments in which we choose the *right* thing. When the big moments of life come, the decisions have already been made.

Iris Murdoch wrote, "At crucial moments of choice most of the business of choosing is already over."[25] Habitual patterns of vice or virtue make it practically impossible to choose otherwise. The battle for our destiny is fought not just in the big moments but in the little decisions we've previously made. For example, a list of taboos may not work at the point when a young man and a young woman find themselves in the back seat of a car. What happens in the situation at hand is a matter of previous thoughts and choices.

Our choices are also influenced by considering their outcomes. Thomas Aquinas said two vices that most obscure the future consequences of our actions are lust and covetousness. We should ask, *What are the future consequences of this choice? What kind of life do I want to live? What kind of person do I want to be? How will the choice I make now affect my destiny later?*

## SUMMARY

Although there is much talk of character in atheistic and New Age circles, these belief systems offer no clear, fixed guidelines by which we can distinguish vice and virtue.

A relationship can rise only as high as the character of those involved.

You can trust someone only to the degree of the person's character that is revealed in whomever they treat most poorly.

Character assumes our actions are not isolated from each other. Each act comes out of our self and shapes our self in an old way or a new way.

Character is formed out of thousands of thoughts, acts and habits.

When big moments come, most of our decisions are already made.

## GOD IS LOVE

*John takes a deep breath and waits for the reactions of the group members. Everyone appears thoughtful.*

*Julia ventures, "I think I see what you mean about this Christ-centered kind of love, this agape love, how it's unique. It does seem different from other ideas of love."*

*Mike says, "The popular idea of love—like in love songs and so forth—seems to me it's all self-centered. As in, what can I get out of this relationship?"*

*Annette looks troubled. "But* shouldn't *we expect to get* something *out of a relationship? Christianity says we should look for what we can give, not what we can get. Okay, but then what happens to* me? *What about what I want?"*

*John suggests, "When the other person in the relationship is asking the same thing, you can see where it causes problems."*

*When Annette doesn't answer, Simon changes to a different tack. "I've heard people say 'God loves you,' but I don't think I've ever heard this idea that God is love. If that's true—well, it can't be true, because there's no God, at least not that kind of a God. But it raises the question, if there isn't that kind of a God . . ." His voice trails off.*

*Mike completes the question. "Then where does love come from?"*

Julia muses, "All this stuff about love and character—it's really interesting. I know New Agers that I'd definitely call people of character. I wonder if they'd agree that their own beliefs undermine the idea of character." She sighs. "I suppose they don't think about it much."

"Thinking can be dangerous," puts in Annette.

"Just like love without character," John concludes.

## 5

# LOVE AND COMMUNITY

## Love Is Never Stimulated
## Apart from Community

*"So am I a safe character?"*

*Simon's question startles John as he settles into his chair. "What do you mean?"*

*"Well, last week you said that love isn't safe if you're a character."*

*"No, no," Annette corrects him, "love isn't safe apart from character."*

*"It's a joke. I—"*

*"John means people need to have some kind of guidelines for right and wrong," Julia puts in. "Otherwise what they call love just becomes a matter of gimme."*

*"You're catching on, Julia. John's going to lose his job soon." This, of course, from Mike.*

*John smiles. "I think we're all learning from each other, which is exactly what should happen in a community. And that's what we're going to talk about tonight—what makes for a lasting community."*

*Mike says, "A lasting community. That's what I was trying to talk about a couple of weeks ago. People always want change. They move all the time for their jobs, uproot their kids. And even if they don't move, they don't stick with anything. Clubs and organizations and things like that—they're dying out."*

"My boyfriend's talking about changing jobs and us moving," Annette says. "I'm not crazy about the idea."

Julia advises her, "You've got to take care of yourself. Think about
what you really need from him. You can't—"

Before they can continue the discussion, John says, "Tonight we're
going to explore the whole idea of community. We're going to look at
the question, Is the cross the only basis on which community can
last? Connected to that is the idea that love is never stimulated apart
from community. The Scripture we'll look at is Hebrews 10:24-25."

Simon asks, "When you say the cross, do you mean the actual cross
Jesus got crucified on? Have they found it? Where is it?"

Julia sits up straighter and says, "Can you imagine the aura around
it?" She holds out both hands, palms outward, and nods solemnly to
John. "It would just radiate love!"

John says, "I'll have to disappoint you, because I don't think anybody knows what happened to the physical cross Jesus was crucified
on. When Christians talk about the cross, we mean what Jesus accom-
plished for us there."

"What's that got to do with love?" Simon asks. "Wait, you mean
Jesus let himself be crucified to show that he loved all humanity.
Right?"

John answers indirectly. "Remember, we described agape as other-
centered, self-sacrificial love. God loved us so much that he gave his
Son to die for us. That's the self-giving love Christ showed on the
cross—and taught us to show each other."

"But what was that you said a minute ago?" Mike asks. "Something
about the cross and community?"

"Christ's death on the cross makes real community possible. The Bible says Jesus has broken down the wall of bitterness between races,
ethnic groups and individuals. Only Jesus calls us to forgive seventy

*times seven—in other words, an unlimited number of times."*

*"How can you say that only Jesus calls for forgiveness?" Simon demands.*

*"In atheism and New Age spirituality there is no basis for evil or sin. So there is nothing to be forgiven."*

*Simon protests, "I've forgiven people for things they've done to me. Maybe not as often as I should, but I didn't need Jesus Christ in order to do that."*

*John replies, "Of course atheists can forgive other people. I'm saying that in atheism there is no necessity to forgive because there is nothing that, strictly speaking, needs forgiveness. It's the same way in New Age spirituality. Remember the basic direction of atheism is inward, toward self-preservation and survival, and the direction of New Age spirituality is both inward and upward but not outward."*

*Annette says, "I'm still not sure about the inward or outward part. How about if you explain it in more detail?"*

## Remarkable Forgiveness

I met Richard Wine when I visited a prison in southern Florida. His story is unique. He came to believe in Christ because of the mother of the man he murdered!

You can imagine Judy Lawson's anger and bitterness toward this man who murdered her son. Judy was a Christian and even involved in prison ministry, but she was consumed by her anger toward Richard. Finally one day she knelt down and gave her anger to God. She prayed that Richard, the killer of her son, would come to believe in Jesus. That was a major victory.

But Judy didn't stop there. She decided to write to Richard in the maximum-security prison where he was serving a life sentence. She wrote something to the effect that she was praying for him and that if he asked for forgiveness for his sins, including the murder of her son, Christ would forgive him.

When Richard got Judy's first letter, he threw it away, thinking she was crazy. But Judy persisted. Over the next five years she wrote occasional letters to the same effect. It started to get under Richard's skin and really bother him. While he spent two weeks in solitary confinement, he decided to read through the Bible. When he got to the book of Isaiah, something started to happen in his heart. By the time he had finished the New Testament, he had committed his life to Christ.

The first thing Richard did when he got out of the "hole" was write to Judy and tell her that he had made the commitment to follow Christ. He wanted her to be the first to know.

Judy decided to visit him in that prison. You can imagine their first meeting, when Richard asked Judy for forgiveness for the murder of her son, and she granted it!

Richard knew that he needed to grow in Christ, so he enrolled in a Bible correspondence course. He didn't know how to type, so Judy would occasionally type his papers. Their relationship developed to the point where she would regularly worship at her church and then drive down to worship with Richard in the prison chapel. As I spoke in the chapel one Sunday morning, the two were sitting together, a visible witness to the power of Christ to reconcile even the worst bitterness.

Just before I arrived at the prison, Judy Lawson had presented a Bible to Richard Wine. Inside the front cover she had inscribed, "To Richard, my beloved adopted son, from your adopted mother."

Only the grace and forgiveness of Christ can do that! When people hear this story, they often say, "I couldn't do that." I don't know if I could either. It took Judy about ten years to get to that point.

All I know is that Judy loved Richard as Christ loved her and forgave him as Christ forgave her. After we have done all the things that sent Christ to the cross, he not only forgives us when we ask but he adopts us into his family.

## A NEW DIMENSION

Jesus' call to forgive and to love even our enemies is an utterly unique characteristic of the New Testament message. In the cross we see the sacrificial love of Jesus, who died not only for his friends but for his enemies, those who were and are in rebellion against his Father.

One author put it this way: "What, then, is the distinctive difference between the Old Testament view of God's love and that of the New Testament? The most obvious and the most important difference—in fact, the only significant difference—is the Cross."[1]

Agape is a vital concept in the New Testament. The belief that *God is love* is front and center. But the key to what love means is seen in Jesus' self-sacrifice on the cross. Leon Morris says, "It is the cross that brought a new dimension to religion, that gives us a new understanding of love. The New Testament writers saw everything in its light, finding their ideas about love revolutionized by what the cross meant."[2]

Perhaps the best-known verse in the New Testament, and the one most often taken for granted, is John 3:16: "For God so loved the world that he gave his one and only Son, that whoever believes in him shall not perish but have eternal life." Jesus' self-giving love is to be the model for our love. Jesus' love not only models but transforms us to be more like him.

For example, husbands are instructed to love their wives "just as Christ loved the church and gave himself up for her" (Ephesians

5:25). The kind of love Christ had for us is not based on our goodness or beauty. This love is poured out for us in spite of our unattractiveness. C. S. Lewis wrote about the husband's love and headship:

> This headship, then, is most fully embodied not in the husband we should all wish to be but in him whose marriage is most like a crucifixion; whose wife receives most and gives least, is most unworthy of him, is—in her own mere nature—least lovable. For the church has no beauty but what the Bridegroom gives her; he does not find, but makes her, lovely. The chrism of this terrible coronation is to be seen not in the joys of any man's marriage but in its sorrows, in the sickness and sufferings of a good wife or the faults of a bad one, in his unwearying (never paraded) care or his inexhaustible forgiveness: forgiveness, not acquiescence.[3]

Sacrificial love, giving until it hurts, is called for not only in marriage but in all our relationships. Jesus told his disciples, "A new command I give you: Love one another. As I have loved you, so you must love one another" (John 13:34). As Christ gave himself for us, we are to give our lives for others.

## NO BASIS FOR LOVE

As we have seen, the direction of atheistic materialism is *inward*. It values autonomy, in which a person declares, "Nobody tells me what to do, not even God." It emphasizes survival and selfishness. Other than arbitrary preference, atheism holds no basis for self-giving love, objective moral values, intrinsic human rights or any meaning or purpose in life. Because there is no evil or sin, there is no need—and certainly no mandate—to forgive.

New Age spirituality holds that we are already perfect and that there is no distinction between good and evil. There is no *other* to love and therefore no necessity to forgive. Ultimate reality and Nirvana are empty, nothing, impersonal, an extinguishing of desire. Other-directed love can hardly be at the center of reality when personality and relationship have no value.

Susan, the former New Age professor, recalls that she did have a community, but it was very superficial, transient, amorphous and philosophic. The people were bound together "by commitments to ecology and niceness." They could not deal with difficult relational issues. You never "put yourself out for a community." Everything was tried in Susan's community: crystals, drugs, sex, even bending spoons! But if difficulties with people arose, you just "moved from one community to another."

## COMMUNITY VALUES

It is currently in fashion to talk about community and its place in shaping our values. But without genuine love, communities fall apart. Unless there are clear, fixed values, it is difficult to identify what things a community holds as important, and therefore it is impossible to pass any values on to the next generation.

We may talk about community values, but there are many different communities and groups with different values. Which community ought we commit ourselves to, and why? Why can't I just create my own community of two or three people and make up my own values?

## THE COMMUNITY OF THE CHURCH

In contrast to atheism and New Age spirituality, the church—the community of Christ—is there to help stimulate one another to love: "Let us consider how to stimulate one another to love and good deeds" (Hebrews 10:24 NASB). The passage goes on to say, "Let us not give up meeting together, as some are in the habit of doing, but let us encourage one another—and all the more as you see the Day approaching" (v. 25). It is clear that the purpose of "meeting together" is not to maintain the church budget or multiply programs but to "stimulate one another on toward love and good deeds" and to "encourage one another." The purpose is also to encourage "confidence to enter the Most Holy Place" (v. 19); to call believers to "draw near to God with a sincere heart" (v. 22); to foster maturity leading to a "full assurance of faith" (v. 22); to encourage the gaining of a good conscience by cleansing the "guilty conscience" (v. 22); to encourage baptism (v. 22); and to call members to "hold unswervingly to the hope we profess" (v. 23). I would say that all these qualities, including love, are never stimulated apart from community. For believers, *community* almost always means a particular part of the body of Christ in the form of a local church.

The Greek word for "stimulate" is *paroxysmos,* and it shows up in the English word *paroxysm.* It means "to provoke, irritate, exasperate" or "stir up." It is a word that communicates intense emotion, and it is almost always used in a negative fashion. When the apostle Paul saw that the city of Athens was full of idols, his spirit was "greatly distressed" (Acts 17:16). But in the context of Hebrews 10:19-25, the word demands a positive meaning. The context of the community *stimulates* or *provokes* love and good deeds. Without the community of the church, love and good deeds are not stimulated.

## MORE NEEDS THAN WE KNOW

Basil, an early church father, argued that "in the solitary life what we have becomes useless and what we lack becomes unprocurable."[4] When we live independently, other people are poorer because they cannot benefit from our gifts. When we isolate ourselves, we are poorer because others' gifts cannot encourage us and stimulate us in the ways we need. C. S. Lewis wrote that we are "one vast need." Yet we spend much of our lives denying our need and being encouraged by others to deny our need as well.

In the film *La Strada,* Anthony Quinn plays a hardened circus performer. A young girl is drawn to him, and they leave the circus together, trying to make a living going from town to town. He treats her harshly, but she puts up with him because she loves him. After a while, he tires of her company and leaves her asleep by the road. When she awakens to find him gone, she is devastated and goes on to lead a sad and lonely existence. Toward the end of the film, the man attempts to seek her out. He arrives in the town where she lived only to find that she recently died. There he also hears about her sadness. He starts saying repeatedly, "I don't need anybody." He even points to the heavens saying, "I don't need anybody." Then he dissolves into tears. It turns out that he had more needs than he knew.

## THE BODY OF CHRIST

The classic New Testament passage on the body of Christ is 1 Corinthians 12. Here Paul addresses two mistaken beliefs: first, that "I am not needed"; second, that "I do not need you."

*I am not needed.* Paul argued that even if you are part of the body that is not as prominent as you would like, even if you think you are unnecessary, you are still needed. All the parts of the body are needed, and need to be functioning in a healthy way, for the body to do well. Perhaps you want to be a hand, but you are a foot; does that mean you are irrelevant? No!

> If the foot should say, "Because I am not a hand, I do not be-
> long to the body," it would not for that reason cease to be part
> of the body. And if the ear should say, "Because I am not an
> eye, I do not belong to the body," it would not for that reason
> cease to be part of the body. If the whole body were an eye,
> where would the sense of hearing be? If the whole body were
> an ear, where would the sense of smell be? But in fact God has
> arranged the parts in the body, every one of them, just as he
> wanted them to be. (1 Corinthians 12:15-18)

When I was speaking at a singles' retreat, I met a young woman
who was convinced that she had nothing to offer anybody. I re-
minded her of the principles of Scripture, that each one has a gift
and that each person is needed. I asked her several questions about
herself and, based on her answers, suggested several ways she
could contribute to other people's lives. I am not sure she was convinced. But we need to be. If you are a believer, you are an important, essential and needed part of the body of Christ! The body will
not thrive or be fully healthy without you. Even if you are in a less
prominent role, others will be poorer unless your gift is used.

*I do not need you.* At the other extreme are those who, in their
own self-sufficiency and arrogance, think they are superior to others and do not need them. Paul countered this faulty idea too:

> The eye cannot say to the hand, "I don't need you!" And the
> head cannot say to the feet, "I don't need you!" On the con-
> trary, those parts of the body that seem to be weaker are in-
> dispensable. (1 Corinthians 12:21-22)

It is easy to regard someone else as less important because of education, status, job, gender, race, socioeconomic level or appear-

ance. Such imagined superiority is smashed by Scripture. We all have needs, and we need to be open to the possibility that someone quite unlike us can meet our needs.

## I DON'T NEED CHURCH

Some Christians say, "I don't need the church; all I need is my fellowship group." It is an often-heard claim, especially from young people of high school or college age or young single adults. Often their attitude is a reaction to deficiencies they have found in churches. Their experience deserves sympathy.

In writing *A Churchless Faith,* New Zealand pastor Alan Jamieson found out that more than nine-tenths of the people he interviewed—people who are without churches—had once been church leaders such as deacons, elders or Sunday school teachers. About 40 percent were once in full-time ministry. Many said they left the church not because they had lost their faith but because they wanted to keep their faith. These findings are not surprising when we consider how many churches are dry and lacking in power and vitality.

David Barrett, author of the *World Christian Encyclopedia,* estimates that there are 112 million Christians worldwide who are outside the church. They make up 5 percent of the total number of people who call themselves Christians. Raymond Brown says this about people who choose to "give up meeting together" (Hebrews 10:25):

> It is because some people have not found within our churches the warmth, care, and concern for which they hoped that they turned away from the organized or institutional churches to religious communities and house

churches, some of them vibrant with more intimate commitment to fellowship and caring.[5]

This phenomenon is not new. John Calvin said this about the
tendency of believers to leave the organized church:

> There is so much peevishness in almost everyone that indi-
> viduals, if they could, would gladly make their own churches
> for themselves. . . . This warning is therefore more than
> needed by all of us that we should be encouraged to love
> rather than hate and that we should not separate ourselves
> from those . . . who are joined to us by a common faith.[6]

German theologian Adolf von Harnack speculated about why
some forsake the assembling together of believers:

> At first, and indeed always, there were naturally some people
> who imagined that one could secure the holy contents and
> blessings of Christianity as one did, those of Isis and the Ma-
> gna Mater, and then withdraw. Or in cases where people were
> not so short-sighted, levity, laziness, or weariness were often
> enough to detach a person from the society. A vain-glorious
> sense of superiority and of being able to dispense with the
> spiritual aid of the society was also the means of inducing
> many to withdraw from fellowship and from the common
> worship. Many too were activated by fear of the authorities;
> they shunned attendance at public worship to avoid being
> recognized as Christians.[7]

## MEETING TOGETHER

Despite all these rationales, Hebrews 10:25 still exhorts the meeting together of believers. The Greek word for "meeting together"

is *episynagōgē*. *Epi* means "in addition to," which may indicate that early Christians worshiped first in the Jewish synagogue and later, in addition, at Christian assemblies such as house churches. Or it may be that believers are simply being urged not to forsake Christian meetings as some were doing. Certainly Hebrews 10:25 does not require a Christian to attend church five nights a week, but it does appear to call all believers to a regular, probably weekly, meeting with other believers.

Critics of the church who depart from it in effect say to the body of Christ, "I have no need of you." They should be aware that to reject a part of the body of Christ is to reject what Christ has established on earth. How can you accept Christ and reject his body?

## Too Much Independence

New Testament house churches were small groups that functioned as local churches, but they did not cut themselves off from other churches or the church universal. The move to replace the church with informal, independent fellowship groups raises several problems. Typically these groups are made up of people of approximately the same age, often very young. Older and wiser people are in effect excluded. Thus, the members often lack an understanding of what is needed for life in Christ, such as in-depth teaching, worship in which our hearts are directed to him according to biblical principles, outreach in word (evangelism) and in action (serving other people's physical, emotional and spiritual needs), the sacraments (baptism and the Lord's Supper) and authority (the offices of elders and deacons), as the New Testament prescribes. If any of these elements are omitted, the people of such a fellowship are to that degree poorer.

We can legitimately find fault with the inadequacy and fallenness of individual churches. When we compare our present day with the New Testament ideal, we have reason for dismay. One writer said that the church is much like Noah's Ark: "If it weren't for the storm outside, you couldn't stand the smell inside."[8] Martin Luther, at the time of the Reformation, was deeply aware of the profound imperfections of the particular churches around him. He said, "Farewell to those who want an entirely pure and purified church. This is plainly wanting no church at all."[9] Any expectation of a perfect church gets in the way of real and good (though not perfect) options in front of us.

IDEALISM STIFLES COMMITMENT

If we do not make a commitment to a particular body of believers, we will never have in-depth community. Unfortunately, idealism can stop us from making and sustaining a commitment to a local body.

I have seen the pattern. First, people join a church thinking that the pastor, the worship and the fellowship are great. They give glowing recommendations to others. After a few years, or perhaps only a few months, they begin to be dissatisfied with the sermons, the pastor and the church leadership, members of the congregation, the worship style or some other fault. They leave and move to another church, where the cycle starts again. They again find the "perfect" church. But again, after a time, it is not perfect either. So they church-hop for the rest of their lives; or, worse, they give up on church.

This is not to say that believers are obligated to stay with one church forever and never change churches. If there are good reasons for leaving a church, by all means go. But realize that if you never commit yourself to a particular body of believers, if you never press on despite obstacles and go through the sometimes painful act of loving fellow believers, you will never have in-depth relationships in community.

Real community requires us to continue to love despite the obstacle of unlovely people. Perhaps we need to forgive, be reconciled and keep giving until it hurts. A difficult church can stimulate us on to love rather than to walk away and become alienated from others. If we stay, we may become God's instruments of reconciliation in that situation.

## AGENTS OF RECONCILIATION

God calls us to be *agents of reconciliation*. If we are to share the message of reconciliation with the world, we need to be a reconciled community. Paul wrote concerning our reconciliation in Christ:

> All this is from God, who reconciled us to himself through Christ, and has given us the ministry of reconciliation; that is, in Christ God was reconciling the world to himself, not counting their trespasses against them, and entrusting the message of reconciliation to us. So we are ambassadors for Christ, since God is making his appeal through us; we entreat you on behalf of Christ, be reconciled to God. For our sake he made him to be sin who knew no sin, so that in him we might become the righteousness of God. (2 Corinthians 5:18-21 NRSV)

Note that *God* is the one who initiates the process of reconciliation. William Temple wrote, "All is of God; the only thing of my very own which I contribute to my redemption is the sin from which I need to be redeemed."[10] Christ, of course, is the one who carries out the task of reconciliation. We are reconciled "through Christ" and "in Christ." Christ, who was perfect, took our sin on himself that we might become righteous in him.

There is a double transfer. Below are two ledger books. One records our sin, and the other records Christ's righteousness.

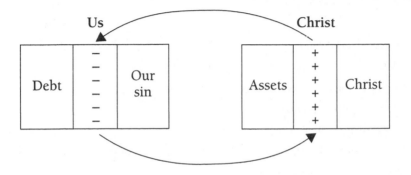

Our sin is transferred to Christ's account, and Christ's righteousness is transferred to our account. Luther put it this way: "Learn to sing to Him and say, Lord Jesus you are my righteousness. You took on you what was mine, you set on me what was yours. You became what you were not that I might become what I was not."[11]

Now not only can we say that we are under "no condemnation" (Romans 8:1) but also that we are righteous! Christ's righteousness covers us like a full-length coat. Now when God looks at us, he sees Christ. There is a sense in which you look as beautiful to the Father as does the Son. There is also a sense in which you are as accepted by the Father as is the Son. How accepted is the Son? One hundred percent. How accepted are you? One hundred percent—in Christ.

Because of what God has done in Christ, we are given a task. We now have a "ministry of reconciliation" (2 Corinthians 5:18); we are entrusted with the "message of reconciliation" (v. 19); we are "ambassadors for Christ" with the new message "be reconciled to God" (v. 20). The only way we can speak the message with conviction is if we ourselves are reconciled. We must be reconciled in order to be reconcilers.

## LASTING COMMUNITY

The cross is the only basis on which community can last because no other religion or philosophy makes reconciliation and forgiveness an absolute necessity. Christ's sacrificial love on the cross impels us to love sacrificially. In Christ's teaching, forgiveness is not optional; it is absolutely necessary.

Right after teaching his disciples the Lord's Prayer, Jesus said these shocking words: "If you forgive others their trespasses, your heavenly Father will also forgive you; but if you do not forgive others, neither will your Father forgive your trespasses" (Matthew 6:14-15 NRSV). One of the marks of being reconciled to the Father is a willingness to forgive and be reconciled to others. If you do not forgive, you are not forgiven.

## EFFORTS AT COMMUNITY

In the 1960s many communes emerged throughout the United States. They were supposed to be all about peace and love, but a familiar pattern developed. Sooner or later an issue would arise between individuals or rival groups that could not be settled. Bitterness escalated until the individuals or groups split off. Then the same thing would happen again to the remnant. The problem was that the communes were often hedonistic, based on the pursuit of personal pleasure. The groups' self-oriented philosophies did not mandate reconciliation or forgiveness. There were many good intentions, but there was nothing that made the painful act of loving a necessity. The philosophy was *inward* toward self rather than *outward* toward loving others as you love yourself.

Some of the communes were based in Eastern religious perspectives. The same pattern occurred among these groups because the thrust of New Age spirituality is *inward* to the supposed divine within or *upward* to merge your identity with that of the One, but definitely not *outward*. It could not be outward because the external world, including other people, was philosophically regarded as *maya,* or illusion. The followers were not motivated to take other distinct people seriously because distinction was regarded as the ultimate lie. Why would you want to reconcile with anyone when you were already One?

Marxism laid out a glorious vision of a utopian community of workers. It was to be *from each according to his ability; to each according to his need.* Why was utopia never realized? The thrust was *outward* to overthrow the ruling classes who oppressed the workers. The end always justified the means. Nothing was prohibited if it led to the good of the masses. Murder, theft, even genocide could be seen as necessary strategies to accomplish the larger goal. Anyone was expendable, which was not an approach that fostered trust. Study the history of Lenin and Stalin (Russia), Pol Pot (Cambodia) or Mao (China) if you want to learn how Marxism works out in practice. Nothing in Marxism necessitates reconciliation and forgiveness.

Other than Christianity, no other religion or philosophy requires reconciliation and mandates forgiveness. No one but Jesus said that if you do not forgive, you are not forgiven (Matthew 6:15). No other religious teacher *requires* that we reconcile with anyone who might have something against us, even if we think it is unjustified, *before* we come to worship God (Matthew 5:23-24).

## FELLOWSHIP AND JOY

How are we stimulated to love and good deeds? Through fellowship. The apostle John wrote, "We proclaim to you what we have seen and heard, so that you also may have fellowship with us. And our fellowship is with the Father and with his Son, Jesus Christ. We write this to make our joy complete" (1 John 1:3-4).

Our fellowship is first with the Father and the Son, which leads to fellowship with each other, which results in *joy*. When there is deep fellowship, there is joy. Conversely, I might suggest that if you are without joy, then you are without fellowship.

Psalm 133 calls the joy of fellowship "good and pleasant" and likens it to precious oil on the head, running down the beard and robe of Aaron the priest. On a number of occasions I have experienced how good, pleasant and joyous Christian fellowship can be. I played trumpet with the Continental Singers and went on tour with them for almost a whole summer. We drove around in our big bus, with about fifty members in the choir and orchestra, performing every day in churches, gyms and concert halls. Sometimes we performed more than once a day, which meant much work setting up and breaking down all the equipment. There was a policy that we had to sit with a different person each day on the bus. Switching seats provided opportunities for each person to get to know each of the others. When we had devotions on the bus each morning, we could share what had happened in the homes in which we had stayed the night before and ask for prayer. Before each concert, we also had a time of prayer and sharing. Sometimes issues came up that needed to be confronted. We had some remarkably honest people on that tour, and our sharing times were not always comfortable. At times virtually the whole group was in an uproar. But by working through our problems, a deep unity and love grew among us.

Our tour left from Los Angeles and went all around the United States, spent a few days on a cruise ship, and culminated in a performance at a hotel in the Bahamas. While we were on the cruise ship, we made friends with those on board, particularly with the band in the ship's nightclub, where we even performed a couple of songs. Many people on the ship were drawn to ask us what we were about because our unity and love were evident. Fourteen people made commitments to Christ through individual witnessing on the ship. One was the drummer in the nightclub band. When we were back in Miami, sitting on the bus and waiting to leave for the rest of our tour, the drummer came on the bus and asked for the microphone. He said, "Thank you for all you have done for me on this trip. I have committed my life to Christ. I have just quit my job. I have decided to go back to England to try to get back together with my wife." There was not a dry eye on the bus. The love and unity of our close fellowship acted as a centripetal force, drawing others to talk to us. We did not have to force conversations into spiritual areas. Out of their need, people were attracted to us to ask about these very things.

The final week of our tour, we drove across the southwestern United States back to Los Angeles, doing concerts along the way. Each person on tour had an opportunity to take the microphone and share what the summer tour had meant to him or her. Because everyone had gotten to know everyone else, we shared a deep bond. That week was filled with emotion, tears often flowing as people shared and expressed their love to others on the tour. It is difficult to express what it was like, but I imagine it was what heaven will be like. We basked in a unity that I have seldom experienced since that time.

From that experience, I drew a few conclusions that have been verified through my study of Scripture and my later experiences. First, if you want community, you need to come together before the Word of God, as we did each day. Second, community is best nurtured not as an end in itself, but in the context of doing the work of Christ in the world. Third, a community is only as unified as the relationships between each of the members. Fourth, expressing our love verbally for each other and verbally encouraging each other is essential to building unity in the body of Christ. Fifth, tough times of conflict and confrontation can lead to reconciliation and deeper unity.

The images in Psalm 133 are along the lines of what I have experienced. Unity is like precious oil being poured on our head. Oil in biblical times signified being set apart as holy, as in the anointing of kings or priests such as Aaron. Fellowship is something holy, set apart, sanctified. Oil in the Psalms also signified joy. Fellowship is surrounded by holiness and joy. It is also abundant and overflowing, like the oil coming down upon the beard and the robes, and the dew of Hermon coming down on Mount Zion. Mount Zion is quite a distance away from the mountains of Hermon. I am told that the mountains of Hermon are lush and have abundant water supplies, while the mountains of Zion are often dry and dusty. Imagine the dew of Hermon dripping on the dry, dusty mountains of Zion. What would the mountains do? Naturally, clap their hands. So do we when the dew of fellowship drips on our dry, dusty souls.

## THE FELLOWSHIP OF THE SON

Christian fellowship is never an end in itself but is a byproduct of our relationship with Christ and the task of reconciliation to which we are called. The night before he was crucified, Jesus prayed for his disciples and for all who would follow him in the centuries to come, including us!

> I pray also for those who will believe in me through their message, that all of them may be one, Father, just as you are in me and I am in you. May they also be in us so that the world may believe that you have sent me. I have given them the glory that you gave me, that they may be one as we are one: I in them and you in me. May they be brought to complete unity to let the world know that you sent me and have loved them even as you have loved me. (John 17:20-23)

Twice Jesus emphasized that the effect of oneness among believers is that the world will believe in him. When believers are not reconciled or not unified, it is a tragedy, not only for them but for the world. The unity of believers is not for the sake of cozy feelings but is a means to show the glory of the Father and the Son to the world.

Fellowship groups can get themselves stuck in a rut. When they come together, they start by sharing their problems. By the end of their time together, things have spiraled down into a depressed state of affairs, and there is little or no time left for Bible study and prayer. This approach is the opposite of what ought to be. We should first focus on Christ and his Word and let Scripture shed its light on our struggles. We will see our difficulties differently when we view them from the perspective of God's eternal truth.

I have seen this in my own experience, not only on the Continental Singers tour but in a Young Life leadership house in which I lived. About ten leaders of the Pittsburgh area Young Life clubs, a high school ministry, lived in two row houses. Every night at 11:00 p.m., whoever was back from their clubs or other ministry work gathered in one of the living rooms. Together we read Scripture, shared insights about the passage and talked about issues that had come up that day or that week. Then we prayed for the kids, parents, teachers and school administrators, as well as for ourselves.

Our times of fellowship were incredibly rich, and prayer flowed with amazing intensity as we praised God, thanked him, confessed sin, and pleaded for our needs and the needs of people we knew. I am convinced that the key to our times of fellowship was that we started with studying the Scriptures. Otherwise our sharing would have been like any secular support group. Only when we come together in Christ will we see his light shed and his power flow.

## THE VALUE OF A MENTOR

In addition to the general value of fellowship to stimulate us to love and good deeds, it is often good to have someone older, wiser and more experienced to hold us accountable and give us insights on how to overcome our particular problems and difficulties. Whether we call this person a discipler, a spiritual director or a mentor does not matter. What matters is that we have a plan to move forward in our spiritual lives, a plan designed with our particular needs in mind. We all have different learning styles, different personalities, different besetting sins, different family situations and different callings. General biblical principles are essential for us to know, but exactly how do they apply to us? That is where a mentor can help.

I have been involved with teaching, discipling and mentoring for six years at the Ligonier Valley Study Center and for twenty years at the C. S. Lewis Institute in the Washington, D.C., area. I have had numerous regular meetings with individuals, lasting up to ten years in duration, although usually shorter. I have also worked with two groups for a year at a time: the Falls Church Fellows, made up of post-college young adults, and the C. S. Lewis Fellows, made up of mid-career professionals.

It has become clear to me over time that there is a definite need for discipleship in the body of Christ, and that the local church is largely unable or unwilling to provide it. I have found especially that young people are not specifically prepared to be disciples in their professions and that professional people are desperate to know how faith in Christ relates to their work, whether in politics, business, law, medicine, science, education or wherever God has called them to serve. In *Christianity and Real Life,* William Diehl writes:

> I am now a sales manager for a major steel company. In the almost thirty years of my professional career, my church has never once suggested that there be any type of accounting of my on the job ministry to others. My church has never once offered to improve those skills which could make me a better lay minister, nor has it ever asked if I needed any kind of support in what I was doing. There has never been an inquiry into the types of ethical decisions I must face, or whether I seek to communicate my faith to my co-workers. I have never been in a congregation where there was any type of public affirmation of a ministry in my career. In short, I must conclude that my church really doesn't have the least interest in whether or how I minister in my daily work.[12]

What is missing? Accountability, development of ministry skills, support, help in making ethical decisions, encouragement to evangelize and affirmation of a God-given calling to professional life. Diehl's evaluation has proved true in my own experience.

## A CAST OF THOUSANDS

Stimulating one another to love and good deeds requires the involvement of many diverse people. It is good to have a mentor and an accountability group, but it takes exposure to the whole body to grow into what Christ wants us to be. One counselor referred to it as a cast of thousands. Each person sees a different side of us, brings out different aspects of who we are and can suggest solutions from different areas.

For example, I have worked as a spiritual director alongside a counselor. I would focus on spiritual issues, and he would focus on therapy. Everyone needs close relationships with family and friends; a sense of physical well-being from adequate sleep, exercise and nutrition; and a sense of who they are as a man or a woman. Different people—a personal trainer, nutritionist, medical doctor or psychiatrist—can help in these different areas. All of them need to be mobilized and asked to participate in the process of discipleship, knowing that the sole weight of another's growth does not rest on each of them alone.

## SUMMARY

Atheists and pantheists may talk of community, but they have no necessary principles that bind a community together. Their thrust is *inward,* or *inward and upward,* but not *outward* to value either the personal or the corporate.

Neither atheism nor pantheism has any mandate for forgiveness because neither has any basis for sin.

Community in Christ stimulates love.

We cannot live our lives in isolation; we need each other.

We are to be agents of reconciliation and ambassadors for Christ.

Stimulating one another to love requires the involvement of many diverse people.

## REASON AND POWER

*Mike takes a long swig of coffee and grimaces. "Cold," he announces. "Guess I've been too busy listening." He sets down his cup. "This community thing—I've seen several sides of it. I've been a member of the same church for over thirty years. We used to have the kind of community you talked about, John. Then we went through a split, and about one-third of the people left the church. A few have come back, but the rest . . . well, it still bothers me. I guess I'm still kind of mad about what those people did."*

*This is a long comment for Mike. Simon immediately asks, "What about this reconciliation in Christ that John talked about? Didn't it work?" He sounds more disappointed than belligerent.*

*Mike ponders a moment. "Some people in the church tried to reach out to the ones who had left. I felt like I should go see some of them too. But, well, I never got around to it."*

*Annette asks, "Why didn't you all just forgive each other? I mean, if you're a Christian, you're supposed to forgive. From what John says, it sounds like you have to." She looks at John. "Right?"*

*John nods. "I'm the first to admit that Christians don't always practice forgiveness, but yes, you're right. If you're part of a community, any community, there's always going to be something to forgive. But Christians are the ones who have a reason to forgive. And we have the power of Christ to help us do it."*

*Simon admits, "As an atheist, I can't say I've ever been part of a community like John talked about. For one thing, there just aren't that many of us. There are online groups where we discuss our beliefs, but I can't say I get regular support or encouragement from other atheists."*

Julia adds, "I've been in several groups where I've felt love and acceptance, but it's never lasted very long. Somebody gets mad at somebody, or people have disagreements over their ideas, and the group breaks up and goes in different directions."

"Maybe it's because they don't have a reason to stay and work things out," John suggests. He thinks he hears Annette mutter, "Stay and work things out?" But she doesn't speak up, so John continues. "That's why a Christian community is different, at least when it's functioning as Christ wants it to function."

Half mocking and half serious, Julia says, "Maybe I should try going to church."

Simon instantly reacts. "You talk about that like it's easy! If I made a decision like that, it would change everything in my life." He looks around the group. "The rest of you don't have any concept of what that means."

John says, "Simon, you may have a better concept of commitment to Christ than a lot of churchgoers have. If a person decides to accept Christ and follow him—that's earthshaking. It's life-shaking. And yes, it can be scary."

Annette says, not very loudly, "I'm starting to think Richard is scared of commitment."

John says, "You know, there's a Scripture that talks about fear and love. Next week we'll take a look at it. I think it'll be helpful for all of us."

# LOVE AND COURAGE

## Love Is Never Seized
## Apart from Courage

*The following week Annette arrives first. As soon as she approaches
the table in the corner, she asks John, "Did you say we're going to talk
about fear and love this week?" John nods and she goes on, "Because
I'm scared of what's going on with Richard and me right now. He says
he loves me, but he also says—" She breaks off her sentence as Julia
arrives, eating a large, jelly-filled doughnut.*

"Iwz wkn lt. Mffdd dnr," Julia says.

Simon, not far behind Julia, says, "Don't talk! You'll choke. Hi,
everybody. Hey, where's Mike? Isn't he coming tonight?"

*John says to Annette, "I hope the discussion tonight will be helpful."
But he wonders if she needs more than that. Her young love relationship seems to be in crisis.*

*Julia manages to swallow her mouthful of doughnut and interpret
her previous comment.* "I was working late and missed dinner."

Simon asks Julia directly, "So, did you go to church last Sunday?"

"Well, I thought about it," *Julia responds, wiping her sticky hands
on a paper napkin.*

"A little too scary, huh?" *suggests Simon.* "I'll bet Annette here went
to church." *Annette doesn't answer, but Simon and Julia don't notice be-*

*cause they are looking around for Mike. John is wondering about him too. Then John sees Mike approaching the coffee counter. John is gratified to feel the group relax when Mike appears.* They've all become important to each other, *he thinks.* And important to me.

*"How's everybody?" Mike asks as he sits down. He immediately turns to John and says, "You know, I realized something this week. Remember I said I didn't go to see those people who left our church? I told myself it wouldn't do any good, or they wouldn't listen, or somebody else should do it and so forth. Well, I've decided there's just one reason I didn't do it. I was scared to! I didn't know how they'd react. So it was safer to do nothing."*

*He leans back and stretches his legs in front of him, at least as far as the table allows. "So, John, what's this Scripture about fear and love that you talked about?"*

## DIFFERENT KINDS OF NEEDS

In his book *Maker of Heaven and Earth,* Langdon Gilkey sets forth the conditions necessary to have a sense of meaning in life. First, we must have hope that our physical needs, such as housing and food, can be met. Second, we must have hope that our emotional needs for relationships, intimacy, love, a sense of dignity, meaningful work and community can be met. Third, we must have a sense that our individual lives play a part in an overarching purpose or destiny.[1]

Science and technology can attempt to meet our physical needs. Psychology can try to address our emotional needs. We can attempt to create our own individual or corporate meaning for life. However, without an adequate spiritual perspective—a relationship with God and an understanding of his purpose and calling for our lives—it is difficult, if not impossible, to maintain a sense of personal wholeness. If all three of these areas are lacking, we have a crisis that can lead to hopelessness and despair about the future. Our fears and anxieties dominate us; courage evaporates.

## ATHEISM: NO REASON FOR HOPE OR COURAGE

Where can we find a basis for hope and the courage to conquer our fears? Does atheism or pantheism give us a foundation for hope or courage? I think the answer is *no*.

Within the atheist perspective, there is no definite meaning for life. We have only our personally constructed meanings. Atheists such as Sartre, Camus, Russell and the writers of the Theater of the Absurd (Beckett, Ionesco, Genet, etc.) have even preached meaninglessness and nihilism. They say that there is no ultimate basis for hope. The best we can expect is some temporary, fleeting connection with people or things, which may give us an ephemeral sense of hope.

In such a philosophy of despair, we can choose to be courageous or not. We can fight or flee; we can shake our fists in rebellion at the abyss of meaninglessness or plunge into despair. Ultimately it makes no difference. There are no reasons to be courageous. There are no necessary mandates to make courage better than despair.

## THE NEW AGE: THE UNDERMINING OF HOPE

In the New Age perspective, there is much talk of hope. Despite the talk, the philosophy itself undermines hope. This system of belief promises a New Age, an Age of Aquarius marked by peace and unity. At the same time, New Age spirituality maintains the emphasis that there is no time, space or matter. It is all One. There are no distinctions between past, present and future.

George Leonard, in *The Transformation,* writes that in the Hindu perspective, "all things are experienced as identical, eternal, and ecstatic."[2] He quotes a Zen philosopher who says, "Nighttime and daytime are not different. The same thing is sometimes called nighttime and sometimes called daytime. They are one thing."[3] Marilyn Ferguson, in *The Aquarian Conspiracy*, is emphatic that there is no time. She says we are victims of our cultural "mono-chronic" linear time. She wants to establish a new paradigm of "polychronic" nonlinear time.[4] This idea could be described as cy-clical time, and it is not new. Augustine addressed it long ago: "They have asserted that these cycles will ceaselessly recur, one passing away and another coming . . . the things which have been and those which are to be coinciding. And from this vicissitude, they exempt not even the immortal soul that has attained wisdom, consigning it a ceaseless transmigration between delusive blessed-ness and real misery."[5]

Nonlinear, cyclical time leaves no place for a real past, present or future. But if there is no future, there is nothing to hope for and nothing really new. There can't even be a *New* Age. If there is no hope and no future, then there is no need to overcome fear and anxiety through courage because there is nothing to cause fear and anxiety. There is no need for courage unless there are real dangers and threats that can happen in a real future.

## THE BIBLE AND THE FUTURE

I once hosted a Bible study for some New Age leaders. The topic was the Bible and the future. In particular, I contrasted the bibli-cal view of time with the New Age view that there is no time—no past, present or future. I pointed out that their view had no basis for anything new, no basis for hope and no resources to equip us to face our fears of the future. They had no answer to what I said, but thanked me for discussing the differences.

When I asked Susan about her former New Age perspective on courage, she responded that there was no courage whatsoever. Courage, she said, implied "a fight." The issue was simply one of harmony or disharmony. There was a sense in which "nobody was against us." There was a fear of "not being accepted" or of "being found out," but the fear was supposed to disappear if you were in harmony with the One. She never considered the idea that love needs courage.

## LOVE IS RISKY

Love requires courage because love is a risky proposition. You might get hurt. It seems safer to walk away from loving. Over the long haul, it appears much easier to *not* love rather than to love.

We may start out with a passion to love, but the bumps and bruises of life dull our desire. It is too easy to allow our passion to be tamed by time. To continue in loving requires all the elements we have studied here thus far: commitment, conscience, character, community and courage. You do not just drift into loving your neighbor or your enemy as yourself. You have to seize opportunities to do so. It takes proactive passion to seize the moment and demonstrate Christ's love.

## SPIRITUAL ENTROPY

The law of entropy exists not only in the universe but also in our spiritual lives. Things tend toward disorder. If you do nothing, you do not stay the same; rather, you decline. If you do not create order, chaos ensues.

The biblical character of Solomon is a classic case in point. He started well, but he did not listen to or remember his own advice.

He had said, "Stop listening to instruction, my son, and you will stray from the words of knowledge" (Proverbs 19:27). But then Solomon allows his wives to lead him into compromise with idolatry in the worship of foreign gods. Apparently he lacked the courage to say no to his wives' yearnings for the idols of their homelands.

Although Solomon had never heard of the law of entropy, he allowed it to rule his spiritual life. He began well but compromised later. Unless we continually seize opportunities to express our love for God and others, we will drift away from doing so.

The law of entropy also applies to love. In the New Testament book of Revelation, the first and last letters to the churches speak to this issue. Christ warns the church at Ephesus, "You have forsaken your first love" (Revelation 2:4). The church at Laodicea had lost whatever passion they once possessed, so Christ calls them "lukewarm—neither hot nor cold" (Revelation 3:16). Both these churches were called to repent in order to go back and recover their earlier love (vv. 2:5; 3:19).

## ACTION IN SPITE OF FEAR

Life contains plenty of things to fear: rejection, failure, disease, war, terrorism and death in whatever form it comes. We would not need courage if we did not have fear. Courage does not mean that we have no fear but that we act in spite of it.

Recently I spoke with a perceptive woman from Africa who at one time had studied in the United States and now teaches jurisprudence in her home country. While back in the States for a visit, she observed that there had been a profound shift in the mentality of Americans since September 11, 2001. She perceived the specter of fear that drifted in the air, altering the American psyche. She said that in Africa there is certainly much to fear, but the threats are so constant that people go beyond them. For people in the United States, the threat was new and vivid. We had been so accustomed to a sense of safety and security that the new possibilities for evil gave fuel to our fearful imaginations. That feeling of fear has waned since then, but it would not take much to rekindle it.

A little saying puts fear into perspective:

> Worriers feel every blow
> That never falls
> And they cry over things
> They will never lose.[6]

Søren Kierkegaard writes, "No Grand Inquisitor has in readiness such terrible tortures as anxiety."[7] How can we be free from fear and have the courage to live for the truth in our times?

Jesus says, "If you hold to my teaching, you are really my disciples. Then you will know the truth, and the truth will set you free" (John 8:31-32). Jesus exhorts us to continue in obeying his words. Obedience leads both to knowing the truth in an experiential way and to freedom. We can experience genuine freedom from fear, anxiety and worry. We need to continually meditate on the biblical teaching on these issues and put them into practice so we *know* them to be true. Only then will we be free to act courageously.

## GOOD FEAR, BAD FEAR

Not all fear is bad! There are three kinds of fear: (1) natural fear, (2) sinful fear and (3) religious fear. The first and the last are good, not bad. Natural fear has a life-preserving value. People who show a lack of fear also live shorter lives. When we are threatened, our bodies mobilize: the heart beats faster, we breathe more deeply and

adrenaline starts pumping. We are prepared to fight the threat or
else flee from it.

Natural fear turns into sinful fear when it becomes excessive or
immoderate. It becomes excessive or immoderate when, in false
hope, we give someone or something the power to help us or hurt
us. Such power should be given to God alone.

For example, when we give someone the power to rule our
thoughts, determine our attitudes or control our actions, in effect
we make that person into a god. We desire that person's approval
more than God's approval. We fear that person's disapproval more
than God's disapproval. The same is true for a circumstance or a
cultural threat that we allow to control us.

## THE ANTIDOTE FOR FEAR

The antidote for sinful fear is the last kind of fear—fear of God.
Long ago the prophet Isaiah wrote:

> The LORD spoke to me with his strong hand upon me, warn-
> ing me not to follow the way of this people. He said:
>
> "Do not call conspiracy
>     everything that these people call conspiracy;
> do not fear what they fear,
>     and do not dread it.
> The LORD Almighty is the one you are to regard as holy,
>     he is the one you are to fear,
>     he is the one you are to dread." (Isaiah 8:11-13)

We should not allow conspiracy theories to control us or determine our attitudes and actions. We are to counter the lesser fear of
conspiracy with a higher fear, the fear of the Lord.

According to Luther, the fear of the Lord is not a "servile" fear, such as a prisoner's fear of a jailer who punishes any infraction with a harsh beating. Instead, Luther called it a "filial" fear, the kind of fear a son or daughter might have of a loving father or mother. Filial fear is not the fear of harsh punishment or rejection but the fear of proving ungrateful for the love given to us or of causing emotional distance between the one so loved.

There is even a fear that can rise out of forgiveness. The psalmist prayed to God, "With you there is forgiveness; therefore you are feared" (Psalm 130:4). The idea seems absurd. We could understand fear coming from an encounter with God's wrath, holiness or justice. But why should fear emerge from his forgiveness? Forgiveness leads to fear because when God shows us such mercy, it would be the height of arrogance for us to take it for granted. How can we be ungrateful for such love and forgiveness? His love should make us anxious to please him.

The book of Proverbs tells us more about this kind of fear: "The fear of the LORD is the beginning of wisdom" (9:10). "The fear of the LORD is the beginning of knowledge" (1:7). We are exhorted to "always be zealous for the fear of the LORD" (23:17). The book of Ecclesiastes, after proclaiming that much of what we deem important is actually vanity, gives us one thing that is not in vain: "The end of the matter; all has been heard. Fear God, and keep his commandments; for that is the whole duty of everyone" (12:13 NRSV). The proper kind of fear keeps us humble, reverent and teachable.

## THE POWER OF FEAR

Jesus knows the power fear has over our actions. In the parable of the talents, the man who was given one talent goes out and buries it in the ground rather than investing it. Later the man admits that he was motivated by his fear of the master (Matthew 25:25). Jesus knows that fear stifles initiative, drains courage and makes us refuse to venture out with God.

In Jesus' parable of the sower, the seed that falls among the thorns is "choked by life's worries, riches and pleasures" and does not mature (Luke 8:14). Jesus knows that worry chokes growth. People bear no fruit because they become consumed with riches and pleasures and are tyrannized by their worries over losing these things.

Jesus also knows that worry causes excessive, anxious activity. When he was at the home of sisters Mary and Martha, Martha was frantically running around taking care of the details of the meal. She resented Mary's passive lack of involvement, as Mary was sitting at Jesus' feet and listening to him. Martha finally burst out, "'Lord, don't you care that my sister has left me to do the work by myself? Tell her to help me!' 'Martha, Martha,' the Lord answered, 'you are worried and upset about many things, but only one thing is needed. Mary has chosen what is better, and it will not be taken away from her'" (Luke 10:40-42). Martha's excessive, anxious activity was motivated by worry, and it kept her from focusing on what was truly important. Jesus was right there, but she was focused on externals rather than on the one thing necessary, Jesus himself.

In the same way, we can let ourselves get distracted and diverted from what is truly important. We frantically run around doing our jobs, seeking power and money, raising our kids and even pursuing ministry opportunities. Yet so often we miss our real focus: Jesus. Perhaps we are afraid to slow down and learn from him for fear of what he will say to us. Mary stopped and listened to her Lord's words. We also need to stop and listen to the Word.

## STOP! THINK! TALK!

When fears overwhelm us, we need to stop *listening* to ourselves and start talking to ourselves. Rather than sitting and listening to the fears and anxieties that inflame our imagination, we need to say to ourselves, "Stop! Don't think that way! Don't you remember God's promises? Don't you remember God's Word?"

Jesus gives us solid reasons *not* to be anxious. Jesus does not just say something like "hakuna matata," the refrain offered throughout the film *The Lion King*. I asked my younger son, Jonathan, then age seven, what the phrase meant. He immediately responded, "It means no worries." He continued, "But Dad, Timon and Pumbaa have all kinds of worries. They are chased by tigers and burnt up by lightning bolts." My son knew that despite the jungle animals' carefree philosophy, the reality of life was different. Instead of casually saying, "No worries," Jesus gives us substantial reasons to counter our fears.

In the Sermon on the Mount, Jesus had a great deal to say about anxiety (Matthew 6:25-34). He gives reasons why we should not be anxious. First, he argues from the greater to the lesser. If God has given us life, will he not give us food to sustain that life? If God has given us bodies, will he not give us clothes to put on those bodies? Then Jesus argues from the lesser to the greater. Consider the birds; they do not plant or reap crops, yet the Father feeds them. If you are greater than the birds, do you not think God will feed you? Or consider the lilies; they do not work, but the Lord clothes them gloriously. The Lord even adorns the grass in the fields. If you are greater than the lilies or the grass, do you not think God will clothe you?

You might respond, "But I have seen dead birds and crushed lilies and burnt grass; what about that?" Jesus shows us the useless-

ness of anxiety even in cases such as these. "Who of you by wor-
rying can add a single hour to his life?" (Matthew 6:27). The
question can be translated two ways. The last phrase can mean
"life span" or "height." In the second case, Jesus would be saying
that anxiety cannot add the length of a cubit (approximately
eighteen inches) to your height. Not many people would be worried about getting that much taller. Maybe someone like NBA
player Earl Boykins, who is five feet, five inches tall, might desire
the height of Shaquille O'Neal at seven feet. But if that is what this
verse is talking about, it would not apply to most people. Sometimes the Bible uses a measurement of length to speak about
length of time. David writes in the Psalms, "You have made my
days a mere handbreadth" (Psalm 39:5). In other words, our days
are relatively short. Jesus says that worry cannot add a single
month, week, day, hour, minute or second to your life span. If
your time is up, anxiety will not extend it. This concept is a com-
fort when we consider all the threats to our life, such as terrorist
attacks. If you are at ground zero of an attack, you will likely die—
but the likelihood of your being there is extremely small. Worry-
ing about these or other threats to your life will not add to the
number of your days.

Jesus went on to say that our Father knows exactly what we
need. If we "seek first his kingdom and his righteousness," then
"all these things will be given to you as well" (Matthew 6:33). If we
put first things first, then our Father will take care of the secondary
things. We are not to be anxious about tomorrow because "each
day has enough trouble of its own" (Matthew 6:34).

In fact, if we are too focused on tomorrow, we will miss doing
what we need to do today. Anxiety about tomorrow could even
bring about the very things we fear today. The more a person fears

doing poorly on a test, the more likely it is she will do poorly. The more a person fears forgetting his lines in a play, the more likely it is he will forget. If you are too anxious during a job interview or on a date or in an important meeting, your fear will cause you to act unnaturally, producing the very rejection you fear.

## FEAR AND LOVE: OPPOSITES

Perhaps the number one cause of anxiety for many in the United States is public speaking. Your audience is free to judge not only the content of your speech but your manner, style and appearance. We know how critical people can be, which makes it a fearsome prospect to stand in front of them.

At one point in my life, fear of public speaking almost kept me out of the ministry. During my senior year at Seattle Pacific University, I was chair of the elections board. I had to get up in front of each assembled class to make announcements about the election procedures. I almost could not do it. I nearly got sick each time I had to give the short announcement. Gradually I learned to overcome my fear. One thing that helped was the promise of 1 John 4:18: "There is no fear in love. But perfect love drives out fear."

Fear and love are opposites. Fear is self-centered, but love is other-centered. Fear is inwardly directed, but love is outwardly directed. Fear says, "If I fail here, it would be the worst that could happen to me." Love says, "Give other people what you have to give."

Whenever I had to teach or give a sermon, I would ask myself, "Do I have something worthwhile to give the people here?" If I did not, I became afraid. But usually the answer was, "Yes, I have something of value. God's Word will not return void." Then I would pray to have a love for the people I was addressing so I could speak in a way that was helpful to them. I would pray over and over, *Give me love for the people I'm about to talk to.* Getting my eyes off myself, not taking myself too seriously, and being willing to look like a fool all came together as I was willing to love. The more love I had for people, the less I feared. I often tell my sons that the best way to be popular in school is not to worry about how you look, but to care for, listen to and affirm your classmates. Get your eyes off yourself and focus on others!

## A SPIRIT OF POWER

Another great help for me in overcoming fear was realizing the power I had available to me through the work of the Holy Spirit. Paul's young protégé Timothy apparently had a problem with fear. Paul wrote to him, "God did not give us a spirit of timidity, but a spirit of power, of love and of self-discipline" (2 Timothy 1:7). So each time I spoke, I asked for a special filling of the Holy Spirit. I prayed for an anointing so that the words I spoke would be burned upon people's hearts, minds and consciences.

When I did seminars for Prison Fellowship, I would often be in a prison for three consecutive days, ministering twelve hours a day. When I arrived each day, as the prison door closed behind me, I had the sense that the power of the Holy Spirit went before me. Even though I was primarily there to teach believers about following Christ more closely, there was not one seminar out of approximately thirty that someone did *not* come to believe in Christ!

Once the leading Satanist at the prison I was visiting came to my talk on Saturday night. I was speaking about faith. He later said that he came because he realized how much hostility he and the followers of other religions directed at Christians. He began to wonder whether Christ just might be the truth after all, and he decided to investigate. At the end of my talk, he told me that he had committed his life to Christ. He wondered what to do next. I told him to go and tell one of the small groups that were now meeting for discussion about the commitment he had made. He did exactly that. The next morning I asked him to share his newfound faith with everyone there. He did and was received with open arms by the believers, who were amazed that one so hardened could be changed. Since the conversion of Saul of Tarsus, who was the greatest persecutor of the church but later became the apostle Paul, such transformations have been happening by the Spirit's power.

At another prison seminar, I noticed a muscular man in a white T-shirt sitting toward the back. His arms were covered with tattoos, and he sat back with his arms and legs crossed. I said to myself, *There is a closed person if I ever saw one.* But as he continued coming throughout the course of the seminar, I noticed that his body language became more open and the scowl on his face lessened. I did not talk to him until the seminar was over. When I saw him walking up the center aisle, I braced myself, not knowing what he would say. To my surprise, he threw his arms around me and thanked me for coming. I could only thank God for softening one who had seemed so hardened.

In another prison, a few minutes into my talk, a man raised his hand. I asked him if he had a question. He mumbled incoherently, saying over and over "666, 666." I got the impression that he and a friend were there to disrupt the meeting. I responded emphatically that the number 666 in the book of Revelation is the number of the antichrist but that I was absolutely certain Christ's power was far greater. The other two hundred inmates erupted in vigorous applause! After that experience, I never doubted that the power of Christ could deal with any inmates who were there to disrupt, and that I had many more *for* me—and for Christ—than *against* me.

## THE POWER OF THE GOSPEL

The apostle Paul wrote, "I am not ashamed of the gospel, because it is the power of God for the salvation of everyone who believes" (Romans 1:16). Because the gospel has power, we need not be ashamed. Unless there was the temptation to be ashamed of the gospel, Paul would not have mentioned how to counter it. Time and again—and not just in prisons—I have seen the power of the Spirit working more powerfully than I could ever expect or imagine.

When I lived in the Young Life leadership house, we published a Christian newspaper called *Liberation*. We passed out free copies wherever people congregated, but especially where people were confronting the big questions of life. Sometimes we went to protest marches, sometimes to Three Rivers Stadium, sometimes just to neighborhoods where college students hung out.

Once we heard about a meeting at which student radicals from all over the East Coast would be gathering. The meeting was to be held at Carnegie Music Hall at the University of Pittsburgh. The featured speakers were Renee Davis, head of the Students for a Democratic Society (SDS), one of the most radical groups in the 1960s and 1970s, and William Kunstler, a radical lawyer who had represented notorious clients of that period, such as the Chicago Seven, the Harrisburg Eight, Catonsville Nine, Joana Little, prisoners at Attica and so on.

One member of our Young Life group, Bill Lane, had been to seminary and was a thoughtful, compassionate teacher. Bill wrote a short address to the students asking them to listen carefully to what was being said that night and to ask themselves a number of questions. First, was Kunstler's solution of revolution really radical enough? Even if the structures of society could be changed, something still needed to happen to the human heart to create a society of peace and love. Second, would the use of violent means create a peaceful society? Jesus said that those who live by the sword die by the sword. Unless there are clear values on which to establish a new society, the method of violence might beget more violence. Third, exactly what were the values on which their new society would be established, where did they come from, and why did they think these were better values than the ones being rejected? Fourth, we felt that the answer was Jesus Christ and the values he established. In Christ there is power to change the heart and there are clear moral values on which to establish a strong foundation for personal and public life.

That was the message we printed up on a yellow sheet of paper, to be passed out to all two thousand radicals who attended, along with a copy of *Liberation*. Eight of us stood at the steps of the hall handing out the flyers to all the students entering. Then we went to our saved seats in the front row of the balcony. The stage was empty except for a few chairs, a podium and a few of our flyers, which people had made into paper airplanes and thrown down from the balconies. Only two people, Davis and Kunstler, were on-stage. Kunstler spoke first, giving a rousing talk that brought the students to their feet with fists raised in the air. Then Davis spoke while Kunstler sat down behind the lectern.

On the chair next to Kunstler was a yellow sheet, one of the flyers we had handed out. While Davis gave her talk, Kunstler unfolded the paper airplane and read it, then put it down next to him. About five minutes later, he picked it up and read it again and put it in his inside coat pocket. We were watching from the balcony, and by this time we were determined to talk to him! After the talks were over, we worked our way downstairs, through the crowd and up onto the stage. Many students surrounded the speakers. I heard one of the radicals say to his friend, "Watch out, they are all around us." Stu Boehmig, editor of *Liberation,* was the first to talk to Kunstler. "What do you think of Jesus Christ?" he asked. Kunstler responded, "It is strange that you ask that question, because I have just been reading the Gospel of Matthew and have been wrestling with the values I see there. I was moved by the flyer I just read."

Then Bill Lane firmly but gently and lovingly asked Kunstler some of the questions he had written on the sheet. Is your solution radical enough? Does it really go to the root of the problems? Is violence the way to achieve your goals? What are the values on which you hope to establish a better society? Rather than grandstand to the surrounding crowd, Kunstler answered time and again, "That's a good question; I need to think about that" or "You know, I am struggling with the same issue." The conversation lasted for about twenty minutes. Finally Kunstler said, "I have to go to catch a plane." He turned to Bill Lane, threw his arms around him and said, "I love you."

We went to the park across the street, did somersaults across the hedges and had a prayer and praise meeting right there! The Holy Spirit did more than we ever dared to expect or imagine. I have found that the Holy Spirit is not a spirit of fear but of power.

## FAITH, HOPE AND LOVE

We need faith and hope in order to love. The apostle Paul called the Thessalonian believers to put on armor. However, this was not the same list of armor he gave in Ephesians 6:13-17: the helmet of salvation, the breastplate of righteousness, the belt of truth and so forth. Instead, to the Thessalonians he wrote, "Since we belong to the day, let us be self-controlled, putting on faith and love as a breastplate, and the hope of salvation as a helmet" (1 Thessalonians 5:8). So the armor Paul advised consists of faith, hope and love.

## WHAT IF . . . ?

Fear, anxiety and worry are future-oriented emotions that cause us to wonder, *What if this happens? Or what about that? That would be the worst thing that could happen!* We conjure up numerous scenarios, all of which reinforce our fears. Our future-oriented emotions can drain us of energy and life, even paralyzing us by anxiety and worry.

What we need to counter future-oriented emotions is hope. Biblical *hope* is not wishful thinking, as in the phrase "I hope so." Instead it is "an anchor for the soul, firm and secure" (Hebrews 6:19). It is faith directed toward the future grace that God promises. "Faith is being sure of what we hope for and certain of what we do not see" (Hebrews 11:1). The things we hope for have not yet happened. So how can we be sure that they will? In Greek the word translated here as *being sure* is *hypostasis*, which means "substance." By faith we taste substantially in the present the things that are yet in the future.

Faith is also the conviction of things not seen. The word here translated "certain" is the Greek word *elenchos*, which Aristotle defined as "that which must be true and cannot be otherwise than it is." In other words, it is an axiom. By faith, that which is unseen becomes axiomatic in our lives. The unseen supernatural world becomes as real as the world we see. By hope—that is, by faith directed toward the future—we can put fear, anxiety and worry into perspective. The more we trust in God's promises and the more we trust in the reality of the unseen world, the more our fear and anxiety are kept in check.

## TRAGEDY IN PERSPECTIVE

Still we might ask, "What if the worst happens?" We still imagine the worst scenario possible. *But the worst has already happened. The Son of God died on a cross.* After that, all other tragedy is relative.

Paul wrote, "I consider that our present sufferings are not worth comparing with the glory that will be revealed in us" (Romans 8:18). Christ's resurrection and the future glory that we glimpse in him, as forerunner and pioneer, alter our view of the future. In this life we have to face much sorrow, grief and pain; but if we weigh it on the scale of eternity, it is next to nothing.

The Old Testament psalmist Asaph, after almost losing his faith in God's goodness, came to this remarkable affirmation:

> Whom have I in heaven but you?
> And earth has nothing I desire besides you.
> My flesh and my heart may fail,
> but God is the strength of my heart
> and my portion forever. (Psalm 73:25-26)

To say "earth has nothing I desire" is an astounding statement. It means that in comparison with having the Lord, all else fades into nothingness. Though the psalmist continued to struggle with his flesh and his heart, he knew that God was his "portion." We know that God possesses us, but we can also affirm that we possess God. He is our portion. He is ours. When we possess God, what do we have in comparison to that which we lack? I think it is true to say, "Whoever possesses God has it all."

## SUMMARY

Neither atheism nor pantheism has any substantive basis for hope in the future, and thus no specific resources to foster courage.

It takes courage, faith and hope to love genuinely.

Courage is not the absence of fear, but acting despite it.

Jesus gives specific help to overcome our fears and anxieties.

Fear creates what is feared, but love casts out fear.

## UNIQUE COURAGE

*Julia is the first to speak up. She insists, "I have hope for the future. I always hope that things will turn out for the best."*

*"But are you* sure?*" Annette asks urgently. "How do you know they'll turn out for the best?"*

*"Well, it's just what I believe. From the things John has been saying, I suppose I don't have a definite reason. Maybe it's just my personality, or the fact that things have worked out for me before. But I guess I believe things will work out just because, well, I believe they will."*

*Mike asks, "Isn't that wishful thinking?" Before Julia can answer, he says, "I consider myself a Christian, but I have to say that my attitude is a lot like yours. I like to think things will work out for the best, but I'm not always sure why. The Bible talks about hope, but I see now that I'm more inclined toward wishful thinking."*

*Simon announces, "I've discovered the cure for wishful thinking."*

*After a brief silence, John asks, "What's the cure?"*

*"Unyielding pessimism," replies Simon in a deadpan, and everyone laughs. Then Simon adds, "I am a pessimist by nature. But I have to admit, pessimism isn't exactly courageous."*

*"I want to be hopeful," says Annette in a voice that doesn't sound very hopeful. "I guess it depends on what you hope for. You shouldn't*

hope for what's hopeless. I need to hope for what's really hopeful. Does that make sense?"

After a moment, the others assure her that yes, it does make sense.

Thoughtfully, Julia says, "This idea that hope leads to courage—that's new to me. I don't think I've found it in the spiritual approaches I've explored."

John says, "Christian hope is just one of the many unique aspects of the Christian faith. It's what gives us courage to love other people. Not that we live up to it all the time, but it's available to us."

Julia says slowly, "When I think of all the love my friends in the New Age movement talk about, I wonder if it's wishful thinking too. Hoping—well, not really hoping, wishing—that everybody will be nice to everybody and we'll all live in peace. And then it doesn't happen." She blinks several times as if in surprise. "No wonder our groups break up so easily!"

Annette says sharply, "Don't say those words!"

"What words?"

"Break up."

Simon points out, "That's what this group is going to do next week, right? Break up? Isn't next week our last week?"

There is a sort of stunned quiet in response to his words. Everyone looks at John, who can only nod yes.

# LOVE

## The Ultimate Apologetic

*The next week as the study group gathers, Julia speaks for everyone when she says, "I feel kind of sad that this is ending. It's been wonderful to hear everybody's views and thoughts. I know I've been challenged."*

*Simon adds, "I feel like we've been able to say what we think and not get condemned or rejected."*

*John says, "Thanks! That's the kind of atmosphere I hoped for when we started this discussion. It's not easy to get there, but you've all been willing to listen as well as talk."*

*Mike says, "I know I've enjoyed hearing everybody else's opinions. Sometimes I get stuck in a rut. I need to hear some different ideas. Not that you've all convinced me, of course." He turns to Annette. "I'm sorry your boyfriend never came to our group."*

*So far, Annette has been very quiet, looking down at the table. Still looking down, she says, "He left. He moved out. He's going to take that job I told you about." No one seems to know what to say in response. Annette goes on, "I decided not to go with him. Well, he didn't exactly beg me to go. I thought he loved me, but—" She looks up. "I'm not even as upset as I thought I'd be. You know? Love is weird. Maybe it isn't what I thought it was."*

*Julia asks, "So are you going to keep going to that church?"*

*Annette nods. "I think I'll get more into reading the Bible too. This group has helped me a lot." She looks around. "Even though it isn't exactly a church group." Everyone smiles, including Annette.*

*John knows he has to get started with their final session together. He looks down at his notes. "Can I sum up what we've done here and refresh our memory? You remember that we started out with John 13:35, where Jesus said that people will know his disciples by their love. We've looked at how love is sustained by commitment, guided by conscience, shaped by character, stimulated by community and seized by courage. So now we're ready to pull it all together. We're going to look at a Scripture passage that's similar to the one we started with. It focuses on how people can know the truth about who Jesus is. It's by our unity."*

*Simon asks sharply, "Unity? How can Christians talk about unity when there are all these thousands of different denominations?"*

*"And they're always fighting," Julia adds.*

*Annette nods and says, "In the town where I grew up, there were so-called Christians who wouldn't go in the door of each other's churches because those churches weren't good enough or holy enough."*

*Mike says, "I'd like to defend all churches, but I've already told you how my church went through a split. That was a real mess." He shrugged. "On the other hand, some people in our church have tried to heal the damage. And there's still a lot of love in that congregation."*

*John says, "There are lots of differences among Christians, but there's a lot more unity than you might think. One theologian said that a believer's goal is 'in things essential, unity; in nonessentials, liberty; and in all things, charity.'"*

*"I like that," Julia says. "Sounds poetic."*

*"Most of the seeming disunity is over the nonessentials. In fact, Christians' disunity may even hide a deeper unity." Everyone looks confused at John's statement, so he says, "Let's look at our Scripture*

*passage. It's from Jesus' final words with his disciples, the night before he was crucified."*

## JESUS' PRAYER FOR UNITY

Jesus had already told his disciples that unbelievers would recognize them by the love they would demonstrate (John 13:35). A little later, Jesus twice emphasizes that when his disciples become one, then the world will know that the Father sent the Son. The quality of love Jesus' disciples show will set them apart as utterly unique. Their love will be a means by which the world can know the truth of the gospel. By contrast, if this love is *not* shown, if this unity is *not* demonstrated, then the world may *not* know that the Father has sent the Son. God is certainly free and powerful enough to find other ways of accomplishing his purposes than through our demonstration of love, but God has appointed this love and unity to be a means by which people can know that his message is true. Here is part of what Jesus prayed that night:

> My prayer is not for them alone. I pray also for those who will believe in me through their message, that all of them may be one, Father, just as you are in me and I am in you. May they also be in us so that the world may believe that you have sent me. I have given them the glory that you gave me, that they may be one as we are one: I in them and you in me. May they be brought to complete unity to let the world know that you sent me and have loved them even as you have loved me. (John 17:20-23)

Note that this is Jesus' prayer for his disciples, or more precisely for those who believe in him as a result of his first disciples. It is Jesus' prayer for believers today. He prays that they will be one.

Jesus' startling analogy is the closeness and unity that exists between himself and his Father. The Father and the Son are distinct persons but share the same will and purpose, as well as the same essence. He prays that believers might be one in the same way (will and purpose, not essence), so that the world might believe.

Of course, this unity among believers is not independent of the truth of the gospel. Believers are to show love to all people, but they have spiritual fellowship in Christ only so far as they are united in spirit and in truth. Believers need to be fundamentally united in the God they worship and the message they preach in the world.

## ESSENTIALS AND NONESSENTIALS

There is that which is necessary for faith to exist (*esse*) and that which is necessary for our well-being (*bene esse*) but which is not essential for being a believer. Richard Baxter's dictum was "in things essential, unity; in nonessentials, liberty; and in all things, charity." Things essential are nonnegotiable. Things nonessential can be vigorously debated because they relate to our spiritual well-being, but they do not demand the severing of fellowship. No matter what, all things are to be done in charity.

When believers act uncharitably towards other believers over nonessentials—or even over essentials—unbelievers are offended by the ugliness they see. While each person is responsible for making a choice about how to respond to Jesus, believers can be partly responsible for the unbelief of the world because of how they treat each other.

Jesus reiterated that believers are to love one another in order that the world may *know* that the Father loves them as he loves the Son. If believers are not united in spirit and in truth, then the world may not *know* the truth about Jesus.

## DEMONSTRATING CHRIST'S LOVE

The way believers relate to unbelievers is important, but the way believers relate to other believers is crucial. If we can't treat well those with whom we share unity in Christ, how can we talk about loving our neighbors, let alone our enemies? Our message is inseparable from the manner in which we conduct ourselves, especially toward other believers. Failure to love a fellow believer is failure to demonstrate Christ's love for us. It is also failure to demonstrate the love that is at the core of the cosmos, the loving relationship among Father, Son and Holy Spirit, from all eternity.

## NURTURING LOVE

In our study of love, we have seen the truth of the following points:

Love is never sure apart from commitment.
Love is never sane apart from conscience.
Love is never safe apart from character.
Love is never stimulated apart from community.
Love is never seized apart from courage.

If love is so important to the witness of believers, how can love be nurtured? We have seen that the way to love is through following the path of commitment, conscience, character, community and courage.

Without commitment, love can't be started or sustained. Without conscience, there is no reliable guide for what is loving, and there is no way to deal with our guilt. Without character, loving relationships are not safe. Without community, love is not stimulated. Without courage, love can be seen as too risky.

## FAILURES OF ATHEISM AND PANTHEISM

We have also seen how atheism and pantheism, despite much talk of love, offer little or no basis for motivating and sustaining love. Both atheism and pantheism hold that the universe is impersonal—hardly a good basis for valuing persons. Both atheism and pantheism hold relativistic views of truth and morality, providing no real *ought* and no necessary mandate for love. Both atheism and pantheism lack any inherent basis for forgiveness, since there is no sin to be forgiven. Both atheism and pantheism lack precisely what people need: a justifying reason to be committed to anything or anyone, clear guidelines for conscience, norms to shape character, a mandate to break down walls between people in community and considerations conducive to courage.

Unless there is commitment, love will not be continued. Unless there is conscience, nothing will be prohibited, even in the name of love. Unless there is character, love will be violated and trust broken. Unless there is a radical call to forgiveness and painful, self-sacrificial love, community will fall apart. Unless there is a basis for hope, both courage and love will be undermined.

Once you give up any objective or absolute values, including the existence of God, then there is nothing that can guide love, nothing of infinite value to which we can commit ourselves, no reason for the guilt we all feel and no way to resolve it, no clear basis to order community life and nothing that can ultimately counter our fears.

## LOVE AT THE CENTER

In contrast to the philosophies of atheism and pantheism, Jesus Christ put love at the center of life. Love is the central concern in Christ's apologetic to the world. Both John 13:35 and John 17:20-23 indicate that the world will not know who Jesus is through the means of his ultimate apologetic—love among believers—unless believers demonstrate his love first to each other and then to the watching world.

The New Testament emphasis on agape is utterly unique among world religions. The statement "God is love" (1 John 4:8, 16) cannot be said in any other view of life. The ultimate demonstration of love is the cross, and that is the painful, self-sacrificial, other-directed love to which we are called.

How can believers learn to love in a consistent way? We must commit to the One who is most worthy, our Lord Jesus. We must get and keep a clear conscience. We must learn what kind of character Jesus requires, and follow that path. We must be part of a community where we are stimulated to love. We must risk loving, and encourage others to love. We must periodically evaluate our hearts, motives and actions, resolve to deal with character flaws, restore our consciences, and recapture our first love (Revelation 2:4).

## THE SUMMIT OF LOVE

In Jesus, love reaches its summit. Commitment is required. Clear values are taught. The path is clearly marked out. Grace is given. Love is stimulated. Courage is modeled. Fear is addressed head-on. The only way love is created and sustained is through the path of commitment, conscience, character, community and courage.

Love is the ultimate apologetic. Both theoretically and practically, we know the truth of Christ because of the utterly unique quality of love shown through his disciples.

## HOPE FOR CHANGE

*John leans back, takes a deep breath and looks around at the group. "Well, what do you think?"*

Simon responds first. "I've always thought of religion in terms of fear. People in ancient times were afraid of natural disasters and spirits and so forth, so all these different religions arose. But I think I see now that Christianity is different."

"Why is it different?" Mike asks him.

"I think it's different because—Jesus Christ is different." Simon reacts as though his mouth has never tasted the words Jesus Christ in quite this way. "I can't separate the idea of God from the idea of Jesus. If I believe in one, I guess I need to believe in the other. But I don't really know what that will mean."

"I want to find out more about Jesus," Annette says simply.

Julia says, "I believe in love, and I want my life to be filled with love. Love for other people, love for the world. I can't think of a higher example of love than Jesus Christ. But I'm just not sure—John, can we talk more about all this?"

Mike says, "My basic ideas about Christ haven't changed. But I have to admit, I haven't been as loving toward the people in my church as I should be. I want that to change."

"We all need to change in some way," John says. "Thank God that his grace is available to us! He wants to forgive us, and he wants to give us the strength to forgive and love each other. Julia, I'd be happy to talk with you afterward. Simon, Annette, Mike—that goes for all of you too, if you'd like."

John drains the last of the coffee from his cup. It's cold, but he feels warm inside knowing that he will continue to see these new friends— friends who, whether they realize it or not, have been drawn together by the love of Jesus Christ.

# RECOMMENDED BOOKS

### Relativism and Postmodernism

Adler, Mortimer. *Truth in Religion: The Plurality of Religions and the Unity of Truth.* New York: Collier, 1990. This book shows how Adler moved from paganism to theism, rejecting relativism and pantheism along the way. He later became a Christian.

Beckwith, Francis J., and Gregory Koukl. *Relativism: Feet Firmly Planted in Mid-Air.* Grand Rapids: Baker, 1998. This book not only gives a short critique of relativism but also shows how it has influenced our society.

Budziszewski, J. *What We Can't Not Know.* Dallas: Spence, 2003. This is a fascinating argument for common moral sense.

————. *Written on the Heart: The Case for Natural Law.* Downers Grove, Ill.: InterVarsity Press, 1997. The author gives an exposition of what natural law teaches us.

Carson, D. A. *The Gagging of God: Christianity Confronts Pluralism.* Grand Rapids: Zondervan, 1996. This book gives a thorough examination of postmodernism, pluralism and inclusivism.

Copan, Paul. *True for You, but Not for Me: Defeating the Slogans That Leave Christians Speechless.* Minneapolis: Bethany House, 1998. This is an introduction to how we can address cultural objections to faith.

Erickson, Millard. *Postmodernizing the Faith: Evangelical Responses to the Challenge of Postmodernism.* Grand Rapids: Baker, 1998. An excellent, thought-provoking study of those in evangelical circles who respond with varying degrees of yes or no to postmodernism.

————. *Truth or Consequences: The Promise and Perils of Postmodernism.* Downers Grove, Ill.: InterVarsity Press, 2001. This is the best book yet in providing a readable and thorough survey of postmodernism and how to address it.

Gaede, Stan. *When Tolerance Is No Virtue.* Downers Grove, Ill.: InterVarsity Press, 1993. A balanced response to political correctness and multiculturalism.

Groothuis, Douglas. *Truth Decay.* Downers Grove, Ill.: InterVarsity Press, 2000. This book helps us to understand the different views of truth people hold and how to give a biblical response to them.

Guinness, Os. *Time for Truth: Living Free in a World of Lies, Hype and Spin.* Grand Rapids: Baker, 2000. This is a readable survey of the dilemma of truth in our age, giving many excellent examples.

Kreeft, Peter. *A Refutation of Moral Relativism: Interviews with an Absolutist.* San Francisco: Ignatius Press, 1999. This imaginary dialogue contains many helpful insights and quotes.

Lehman, David. *Signs of the Times: Reconstruction and the Fall of Paul de Man.* New York: Poseiden Press, 1991. A brilliant and fascinating look at postmodernism, the scandal surrounding one of its leaders, Paul de Man, and struggling with how to respond to it.

Lundin, Roger. *The Culture of Interpretation: Christian Faith and the Postmodern World.* Grand Rapids: Eerdmans, 1993. This is an excellent and well-written book on the roots and fruits of postmodern literary theory.

McCallum, Dennis, ed. *The Death of Truth.* Minneapolis: Bethany House, 1996. This book is a helpful collection of essays on the postmodern impact on various arenas of life, such as health care, education, literature, history, law, science, etc.

McDowell, Josh, and Bob Hostetler. *The New Tolerance: How a Cultural Movement Threatens to Destroy You, Your Faith and Your Children.* Wheaton, Ill.: Tyndale House, 1998. Here is a helpful book, one of the few that takes on the tolerance held in our culture.

McGrath, Alister. *A Passion for Truth: The Intellectual Coherence of Evangelicalism.* Downers Grove, Ill.: InterVarsity Press, 1996. This book is helpful in evaluating postliberalism, postmodernism and pluralism.

Middleton, J. Richard, and Brian J. Walsh. *Truth Is Stranger Than It Used to Be: Biblical Faith in a Postmodern Age.* Downers Grove, Ill.: InterVarsity Press, 1995. This book has many helpful insights and leans toward saying yes to postmodernism. (Also see Erickson's helpful summary of pros and cons of this position in *Postmodernizing the Faith*.)

Murray, Michael J., ed. *Reason for the Hope Within*. Grand Rapids: Eerdmans, 1999. Contains many good essays; in particular, see chapters seven and eight on religious pluralism and Eastern religions.

Norris, Christopher. *Against Relativism: Philosophy of Science, Deconstruction, and Critical Theory*. Oxford: Blackwells, 1997. The book is a good refutation of postmodern attempts to use science to support its position.

Oden, Thomas C. *After Modernity—What? Agenda for Theology*. Grand Rapids: Zondervan, 1992. A brilliant look at how the formerly liberal Oden now views the modernism he once held.

Phillips, Timothy R., and Dennis L. Okholm, eds. *Christian Apologetics in the Postmodern World*. Downers Grove, Ill.: InterVarsity Press, 1995. This book provides a wide range of essays on how to shape apologetics in a postmodern world. It has many helpful insights from a number of writers.

Schaeffer, Francis. *The God Who Is There: Speaking Historic Christianity into the Twentieth Century*. Downers Grove, Ill.: InterVarsity Press, 1968. This is a classic book, a must-read for today's generation. The task Schaeffer calls us to is not completed.

Sproul, R. C., John Gerstner and Arthur Lindsley. *Classical Apologetics: A Rational Defense of the Christian Faith and a Critique of Presuppositionalism*. Grand Rapids: Zondervan, 1984. Reading this book may help you formulate the case for absolutes, giving reasons for a belief that there is a God and for the authority of Scripture.

Veith, Gene Edward, Jr. *Postmodern Times: A Christian Guide to Contemporary Thought and Culture*. Wheaton, Ill.: Good News, 1994. This is a good introductory survey of postmodernism.

White, James Emery. *What Is Truth? A Comprehensive Study of the Positions of Cornelius Van Til, Francis Schaeffer, Carl F. H. Henry, Donald Bloesch, Millard Erickson*. Nashville: Broadman & Holman, 1994. A look at the concepts of truth held by American evangelicals, such as Cornelius Van Til, Francis Schaeffer, Carl Henry, Donald Bloesch and Millard Erickson.

Zacharias, Ravi. *Jesus Among Other Gods: The Absolute Claims of the Christian Message*. Nashville: Word, 2000. This is a winsome discussion by a great communicator focusing on Christianity's relationship to other religions.

## New Age and Neo-Paganism

Albrecht, Mark. *Reincarnation: A Christian Appraisal*. Downers Grove, Ill.: InterVarsity Press, 1982. For a biblical response to reincarnation, this is an excellent source.

Chandler, Russell. *Understanding the New Age*. Dallas: Word, 1988. This is a good survey of New Age spirituality up to 1988.

Clark, David K., and Norman L. Geisler. *Apologetics in the New Age: A Christian Critique of Pantheism*. Grand Rapids: Baker, 1990. Here is a great philosophical critique of pantheism.

Copleston, Frederick. *Religion and the One: Philosophies East and West*. New York: Crossroad, 1982. For an outstanding philosophical discussion of the all-is-One philosophy, read this book.

Davis, Philip G. *Goddess Unmasked. The Rise of Neopagan Feminist Spirituality*. Dallas: Spence, 1998. This is an outstanding recent book on Neo-Paganism.

Geisler, Norman L., and J. Yutaka Anano. *The Reincarnation Sensation*. Wheaton, Ill.: Tyndale, 1986. A survey on the issue of reincarnation.

Groothuis, Douglas. *Confronting the New Age: How to Resist a Growing Religious Movement*. Downers Grove, Ill.: InterVarsity Press, 1988. After you understand what the New Age is about, this book helps you confront it.

————. *Revealing the New Age Jesus: Challenges to Orthodox Views of Christ*. Downers Grove, Ill.: InterVarsity Press, 1990. This is necessary reading showing how New Age authors try to incorporate a different Jesus into their views.

Hoyt, Karen, ed. *New Age Rage*. Old Tappan, N.J.: Revell, 1987. Here are helpful insights into various dimensions of the movement (my chapter is the last).

Jones, Peter. *Pagans in the Pews*. Ventura, Calif.: Regal, 2001. This book is an update and revision of his earlier book *Spirit Wars,* showing how Neo-Paganism has infiltrated the church.

Mangalwadi, Vishal. *The World of Gurus.* New Delhi, India: Nivedit Good Books Distributors, 1987. Here is a superb response to Hinduism from an articulate Christian in India.

Miller, Eliot. *A Crash Course in the New Age: Describing and Evaluating a Growing Social Force.* Grand Rapids: Baker, 1990. This is a good introduction to the New Age way of thinking.

Newport, John P. *The New Age Movement and the Biblical Worldview: Conflict and Dialogue.* Grand Rapids: Eerdmans, 1998. Newport's book is a very thorough update on New Age thinking and Neo-Paganism.

Zacharias, Ravi. *The Lotus and the Cross: Jesus Talks with Buddha.* Sisters, Ore.: Multnomah, 2001. Here is a creative dialogue imagined between Jesus and Buddha. The author spent considerable time researching this book by talking to Buddhist monks. It is very helpful in getting to the roots, questions and problems with this significant influence on the New Age movement in the West.

# Notes

Chapter 1: How Will They Know?

[1]For the story of John's previous discusssion group, see Art Lindsley, *C. S. Lewis's Case for Christ* (Downers Grove, Ill.: InterVarsity Press, 2005).

[2]Quoted in Andrew Higgins, "In Europe God Is (Not) Dead," *Wall Street Journal*, 14 July 2007, p. A-1.

[3]Marilyn Ferguson, *The Aquarian Conspiracy: Personal and Social Transformation in the 1980s* (Los Angeles: J. P. Tarcher, 1980), pp. 100, 172, 180.

[4]Deepak Chopra, *The Seven Spiritual Laws of Success: A Practical Guide to the Fulfillment of Your Dreams* (New York: New World Library, 1994), p. 4.

[5]Ibid., p. 3.

[6]Deepak Chopra, *Ageless Body, Timeless Mind: The Quantum Alternative to Growing Old* (New York: Harmony Books, 1993), p. 27.

[7]Andrew Weil, *Natural Health, Natural Medicine: A Comprehensive Manual for Wellness and Self-Care* (Boston: Houghton Mifflin, 1990), p. 150.

[8]Gary Zukav, *The Seat of the Soul* (New York: Simon and Schuster, 1990), p. 111.

[9]For a more thorough look at this idea, see Francis Schaeffer, *The Mark of the Christian*, 2nd ed. (Downers Grove, Ill.: InterVarsity Press, 2006).

[10]The statements about commitment and character were inspired by comments of Dr. Bill White at Ligonier Valley Study Center.

[11]This story about Alexander the Great comes from a talk by James Kennedy.

[12]This anecdote is from a talk given by Dr. Denny McCain at a conference of the International Institute for Christian Studies, July 20, 2006. Recordings are available from IICS by calling (800) 776-4427.

Chapter 2: Love and Commitment

[1]Robert Bellah et al., *Habits of the Heart: Individualism and Commitment in American Life*, 3rd ed. (Berkeley: University of California Press, 2007).

[2]Richard Rorty, "Wild Orchids and Trotsky," in *Wild Orchids and Trotsky: Messages from American Universities*, ed. Mark Edmundson (New York: Penguin, 1993), p. 44.

[3]Richard Rorty, "Human Rights, Rationality and Sentimentality," in *The Human Rights Reader*, ed. Walter Laqueur and Barry Rubin (New York: New American Library, 1993), p. 266.

[4]Shankara, quoted in Os Guinness, *Unspeakable: Facing Up to Evil in an Age of Genocide and Terror* (San Francisco: HarperSanFrancisco, 2005), p. 122.

[5]Ibid., p. 123.

[6]George Leonard, *The Transformation* (Los Angeles: J. P. Tarcher, 1972), pp. 135-39.

[7]See Francis Schaeffer, *Pollution and the Death of Man* (Wheaton, Ill.: Crossway Books, 1992).

[8]G. K. Chesterton, *Orthodoxy* (New York: Doubleday, 1990), p. 41.

[9]Jonathan Edwards, *The Nature of True Virtue* (Ann Arbor: University of Michigan Press, 1969).

[10]Quoted in Jon Meacham, "Pilgrim's Progress," *Newsweek*, August 14, 2006, p. 36.

[11]William Barclay, *The Gospel of Matthew* (Philadelphia: Westminster Press, 1975), 2:151.

[12]John MacArthur, *Matthew 16-23*, MacArthur New Testament Commentary Series (Chicago: Moody Publishers, 1988), p. 47.

[13]Ibid., p. 49.

[14]John Piper, *Desiring God: Meditations of a Christian Hedonist* (Sisters, Ore.: Multnomah Publishers, 1996), p. 9.

[15]C. S. Lewis, *Weight of Glory and Other Literary Addresses* (San Francisco: HarperCollins, 1976), p. 26.

[16]C. S. Lewis, *Mere Christianity* (San Francisco: HarperCollins, 2001), p. 226-27.

[17]There are many Christian organizations devoted to giving answers to the questions skeptics ask. Some provide phone counseling so you can speak to someone who will give you answers and written information as well. One such organization is the Spiritual Counterfeits Project, which focuses on information about cults and new spiritual movements. Their hotline is (510) 540-5767.

[18]For further study on these themes, see "The Characteristics of Cultic Commitment," chapter nine in Ronald Enroth's book *Youth, Brainwashing and the Extremist Cults* (Grand Rapids: Zondervan, 1977). Also see an excellent study by

sociologist Rosabeth Moss Kanter, *Commitment and Community: Communes and Utopias in Sociological Perspective* (Cambridge, Mass.: Harvard University Press, 1972), which focuses on comparing contemporary communes and the more successful utopian communities of the nineteenth century. Another helpful resource, a series of questions to distinguish between cultic and legitimate groups, is found in the chapter by LaVonne Neff, "Evaluating Cults and New Religions," in Ronald Enroth et al., *A Guide to Cults and New Religions* (Downers Grove, Ill.: InterVarsity Press, 1983), pp. 196-97.

[19]The above marriage analogy and the story about Bill Pannell were given in a talk many years ago by the Rev. Dr. John Guest.

### Chapter 3: Love and Conscience

[1]William Barrett, *Time of Need: Forms of Imagination in the Twentieth Century* (New York: Harper and Row, 1973), pp. 224-40.

[2]William Fenner, *Works* (1651), pp. 108ff.

[3]Ibid.

[4]Martin Luther, quoted in Gordon Rupp, *The Righteousness of God: Luther Studies* (London: Hodder and Stoughton, 1953), p. 227.

[5]B. B. Warfield, *Selected Shorter Writings of Benjamin B. Warfield* (Nutley, N.J.: Presbyterian & Reformed, 1970-1973), 2:463-65.

### Chapter 4: Love and Character

[1]Michael Ghiselin, *The Economy of Nature and the Evolution of Sex* (Berkeley: University of California Press, 1974), p. 247.

[2]David Barash, *Sociobiology and Behavior* (New York: Elsevier, 1977), p. 167.

[3]Richard Dawkins, quoted in Henry Plotkin, *Evolution in Mind: An Introduction to Evolutionary Psychology* (Cambridge, Mass.: Harvard University Press, 1997), p. 21.

[4]Charles Darwin, *On the Origin of Species by Means of Natural Selection, or The Preservation of Favored Races in the Struggle for Life* (Cambridge, Mass.: Harvard University Press, 1967), p. 199.

[5]Richard Dawkins, *The Selfish Gene*, 30th anniv. ed. (New York: Oxford University Press, 2006), p. 201.

[6]Richard Dawkins, *The God Delusion* (New York: Houghton Mifflin, 2006), pp. 220-21.

[7]Yun-Men, quoted in Os Guinness, *The East, No Exit* (Downers Grove, Ill.: InterVarsity Press, 1974), p. 40.

[8]Hermann Hesse, *Siddhartha,* trans. Hilda Rosner (New York: New Directions, 1951), p. 116.

[9]Arthur Koestler, *The Lotus and The Robot* (New York: Harper and Row, 1960), pp. 273-74, quoted in Pat Means, *The Mystical Maze* (Campus Crusade for Christ, 1976), p. 63.

[10]Quoted in Leon Morris, *Testaments of Love: A Study of Love in the Bible* (Grand Rapids: Eerdmans, 1981). Ethelbert Stauffer says, "It is indeed striking that the substantive agape is almost completely lacking in pre-Biblical Greek" (*Theological Dictionary of the New Testament,* trans. G. W. Bromiley [Grand Rapids: Eerdmans, 1977], 1:37). The word is not entirely new, but not used commonly prior to the New Testament. New Testament writers took the infrequently used noun *agape,* filled it with new meaning, and placed it front and center in the biblical story. See also Morris, *Testaments of Love,* pp. 123-32.

[11]William Barclay, *The Mind of Jesus* (London: SCM Press, 1960), p. 117.

[12]Ibid., p. 118.

[13]Leon Morris, *Testaments of Love: A Study of Love in the Bible* (Grand Rapids: Eerdmans, 1981), p. 142.

[14]Emil Brunner, *The Christian Doctrine of God* (London: James Clarke, 1949), p. 192.

[15]Ibid., p. 183.

[16]James Davison Hunter, *The Death of Character: Moral Education in an Age Without Good or Evil* (New York: Basic Books, 2000), p. 117.

[17]Ibid., p. 118.

[18]Ibid., p. 120.

[19]Ibid., p. xiii.

[20]Ibid., p.

[21]Ibid., p. xv.

[22]Stanley Hauerwas, *Character and the Christian Life: A Study in Theological Ethics* (Notre Dame, Ind.: University of Notre Dame Press, 1989), p 17.

[23]C. S. Lewis, *Mere Christianity* (San Francisco: HarperCollins, 2001), p. 92.

[24]William Glasser, *Positive Addiction* (New York: Harper & Row, 1976).

[25]Iris Murdoch, *The Sovereignty of Good* (New York: Schocken Books, 1971), p. 37.

**Chapter 5: Love and Community**
[1]Walter Harrelson, *The Journal of Religion* 31 (1951): 173-74.

[2]Leon Morris, *Testaments of Love: A Study of Love in the Bible* (Grand Rapids: Eerdmans, 1981), p. 129.

[3]C. S. Lewis, *The Four Loves* (New York: Harvest Books, 1971), p. 148.

[4]Basil, quoted in Thomas Oden, *Life in the Spirit* (San Francisco: HarperCollins, 1994), p. 282.

[5]Raymond Brown, *The Message of Hebrews: Christ Above All* (Downers Grove, Ill.: InterVarsity Press, 1982), p. 185.

[6]John Calvin, quoted in Brown, *Message of Hebrews,* p. 188.

[7]Adolf von Harnack, *Mission and Expansion of Christianity* (London: Williams and Norgate, 1908), 1:434, quoted in F. F. Bruce, *The Epistle to the Hebrews* (Grand Rapids: Eerdmans, 1990), p. 257.

[8]From a late medieval manuscript quoted in Robert McAfee Brown, *The Significance of the Church* (Philadelphia: Westminster Press, 1956), p. 17.

[9]Martin Luther, quoted in *Christian History Magazine* 34, no. 2 (1992): 28.

[10]William Temple, quoted in John Stott, *The Cross of Christ* (Downers Grove, Ill.: InterVarsity Press, 1986), p. 197.

[11]Martin Luther, *The Letters of Spiritual Counsel,* p. 110, quoted in Stott, *Cross of Christ,* p. 200.

[12]William Diehl, *Christianity and Real Life* (Philadelphia: Fortress, 1976), p. v.

### Chapter 6: Love and Courage

[1]Langdon Gilkey, *Maker of Heaven and Earth* (New York: Doubleday, 1959), p. 159.

[2]George Leonard, *The Transformation* (Los Angeles: J. P. Tarcher, 1972), p. 61.

[3]Ibid., p. 119.

[4]Marilyn Ferguson, *The Aquarian Conspiracy: Personal and Social Transformation in the 1980s* (Los Angeles: J. P. Tarcher, 1980), p. 104.

[5]Augustine, quoted in Gilkey, *Maker of Heaven and Earth,* p. 248.

[6]R. Kent Hughes, *Luke* (Wheaton, Ill.: Crossway, 1998), 2:53.

[7]Søren Kierkegaard, quoted in ibid.

# Index